OXFORD MONOGRAPHS IN INTERNATIONAL LAW

General Editor: Professor Ian Brownlie CBE, QC, FBA
Chichele Professor of Public International Law in the University of Oxford and Fellow of All Souls College, Oxford.

HUMAN RIGHTS STANDARDS AND THE FREE MOVEMENT OF PEOPLE WITHIN STATES

OXFORD MONOGRAPHS IN INTERNATIONAL LAW

The aim of this series of monographs is to publish important and original pieces of research on all aspects of public international law. Topics which are given particular prominence are those which, while of interest to the academic lawyer, also have important bearing on issues which touch the actual conduct of international relations. None the less the series is wide in scope and includes monographs on the history and philosophical foundations of international law.

RECENT TITLES IN THIS SERIES

The Concept of International Obligations
Erga Omnes
M. RAGAZZI

The Termination and Revision of Treaties
in the Light of New Customary International Law
N. KONTOU

Land and Maritime Zones of Peace
in International Law
S. P. SUBEDI

International Management of Hazardous Wastes:
The Basel Convention and Related Legal Rules
K. KUMMER

Human Rights in the Private Sphere
A. CLAPMAN

Self-Determination and National Minorities
T. D. MUSGRAVE

Regime of Straits in International Law
B. B. JIA

Naval Weapons Systems and the
Contemporary Law of War
J. J. BUSUTILL

Human Rights Standards and the Free Movement of People Within States

CHALOKA BEYANI

OXFORD
UNIVERSITY PRESS

OXFORD
UNIVERSITY PRESS

Great Clarendon Street, Oxford OX2 6DP

Oxford University Press is a department of the University of Oxford.
If furthers the University's objective of excellence in research, scholarship,
and education by publishing worldwide in

Oxford New York

Athens Auckland Bangkok Bogotá Buenos Aires Calcutta
Cape Town Chennai Dar es Salaam Delhi Florence Hong Kong Istanbul
Karachi Kuala Lumpur Madrid Melbourne Mexico City Mumbai
Nairobi Paris São Paulo Singapore Taipei Tokyo Toronto Warsaw

with associated companies in Berlin Ibadan

Published in the United States
by Oxford University Press Inc., New York

First published 2000

British Library Cataloguing in Publication Data
Data available

Library of Congress Cataloging in Publication Data
Beyani, Chaloka.
Human rights standards and the movement of people within the states / Chaloka Beyani.
p. cm.—(Oxford monographs in international law)
Includes bibliographical references and index.
1. Freedom of movement. 2. Human rights. I. Title. II. Series.
K3265 .B49 1999 341. 4'81—dc21 99-048740

ISBN-0-19-826821-1

1 3 5 7 9 10 8 6 4 2

Typeset in Times
by Best-set Typesetter Ltd., Hong Kong
Printed in Great Britain
on acid-free paper by
Biddles Ltd., Guildford and King's Lynn

General Editor's Preface

The work of Dr. Beyani represents an addition to the growing number of titles in the *Series* devoted to topics in the sphere of human rights. The question of the movement of people within States tends to be neglected in the literature in spite of its obvious practical importance. The present study provides a comprehensive treatment of this complex issue and will make a significant recruit to the existing library of monographs on human rights.

Blackstone Chambers
The Temple **IAN BROWNLIE**

27 October 1999

Acknowledgements

This book is a substantially revised version of the D.Phil thesis written originally at Oxford in 1992. I drew help, support, and encouragement from many people during the time in which I wrote the thesis and prepared it for publication. While it is not possible to mention all of them here, I have, however, registered my appreciation to every one concerned in a variety of ways.

I am foremost immensely grateful to Professor Ian Brownlie, Q.C., C.B.E., F.B.A., and Chichele Professor of Public International Law in the University of Oxford, for his meticulous guidance and supervision of the thesis upon which this study is based. Of him I have to say, without prejudice, that it is my greatest and sincerest pleasure to have been a pupil of an eminent and leading international lawyer of his generation. But I also owe Professor Brownlie a great debt for his professional help and personal support in many aspects of my academic work, and I fear that I shall never repay this debt in my entire lifetime.

Sincere thanks go to my examiners Professor David Harris of the University of Nottingham and Professor Paul P. Craig, Norton Rose Professor of Law in the University of Oxford, for their kind but thorough examination of my thesis, and for their helpful comments and advice. At the LSE, I extend my equal gratitude and appreciation to Professor Christine Chinkin and Professor Christopher Greenwood for their comments, insights, and suggestions, as well as for their personal encouragement in the final stages of this work. I must thank Amanda Tinnams, my Secretary at LSE, for helping me out with the odd tasks of putting together the 'bits and pieces' of the book.

The Association of Commonwealth Universities deserves special mention, for it was the award of their prestigious Fellowship that enabled me to undertake doctoral studies at Oxford in October 1988. At Oxford University Press my immense thanks are due to Messrs John Louth and Chris Rycroft for their professionalism, sound judgement and help in getting this book through the final stages of publication by the Press.

Many thanks too to Professor Muna Ndulo at Cornell University who greatly stimulated my interest in the study of law at the University of Zambia in 1978, to Professor Henrietta Moore of the London School of Economics, Professor Megan Vaughan of Nuffield College, Oxford, to Professor Stephen Chan at Nottingham Trent University, and George Okoth-Obbo, at the United Nations Higher Commissioner for Refugees, for their continuing friendship, academic support and encouragement throughout the time when I wrote the thesis and developed it into a manuscript for publication. I am also thankful to the staff of the Bodleian Law Library at Oxford for their help in locating materials in the library.

Finally but not least, immeasurable thanks are due to: my parents, brothers and sisters for everything; my wife Vivian for her unfailing help, presence and patience. She has done so steadfastly despite losing both her parents and two of her sisters in the period between the completion of the thesis and the publication of the book. May all their souls rest in peace. And very many thanks to my sons Ntumbu and Puchay for being there when I needed them. This book is dedicated to them in the hope that they and their generation will live in a world in which free movement will have become a reality.

N.B. My father, Maxwell S. Beyani, died on 27th August 1999 shortly before the publication of this book. May his soul rest in peace.

C.B.

Harefields, November 1998

Contents

Abbreviations

ALM	African Legal Materials.
AJIL	American Journal of International Law.
BYIL	British Yearbook of International Law.
ECOWAS	Economic Community of West African States.
EEC	European Economic Community
EU	European Union
IACHR	Inter-American Commission on Human Rights.
ICJ	International Court of Justice.
ICLQ	International and Comparative Law Quarterly.
IGAD	Inter-Governmental Authority on Development.
ILM	International Legal Materials.
ILO	International Labour Organisation.
NAFCO	National Agricultural Food Corporation Agency.
WHO	World Health Organisation.
Recueil	Recueil Des Cours (Collected Courses of the Hague Academy of International Law).
SADC	Southern African Development Community.
UNTS	United Nations Treaty Series.

Table of Cases

1
Introductory

Freedom to move about and to choose a place of residence within States is intrinsically one of the most natural and basic human rights protected by international law. Initial evidence for such protection clearly derives from the Universal Declaration of Human Rights 1948,[1] the first instrument of international scope in the era of the Charter of the United Nations 1945 to establish standards for the protection of human rights, including freedom of movement within and between States.

Article 13(1) of the Declaration stipulates the pertinent standards by providing that: 'Everyone has the right to freedom of movement and residence within the borders of each State'. There is justification for advancing the argument that the inclusion within the Universal Declaration of the right to freedom of movement, both within State territory and for the purpose of entering and leaving it, has given prominence to its status as one of the human rights declared fundamental to all persons.[2] In the case of the incarceration of *United States Diplomatic and Consular Staff in Tehran*[3] the International Court of Justice stated that 'wrongfully to deprive human beings of their freedom and to subject them to physical constraint in conditions of hardship is in itself manifestly incompatible with the Charter of the United Nations as well as the fundamental principles enunciated in the Universal Declaration of Human Rights'.

There can be no prize for guessing that the confinement of American diplomats who were taken as hostages in this case constituted, amongst other factors, deprivation of liberty and infringement of their freedom of movement.

The special importance attached to the free movement of persons has been evident from the beginning of the very process of elaborating the modern concept of human rights in international law. In addition to the weight of the Universal Declaration, the preparatory work to the International Covenant on Civil and Political Rights 1966 supports the view that the right to freedom of internal movement and residence was included in it because it 'constituted an important human right and one which was an

[1] U.N. Doc. A/811.

[2] Goodwin-Gill, *International Law and The Movement of Persons Between States* (Oxford, 1978), 20.

[3] *United States v Iran* (1980) I.C.J. Rep., p.1 para. 91.

essential part of the right to personal liberty'.[4] During the preparation of the European Convention for the protection of Human Rights and Fundamental Freedoms 1950 the drafting committee accepted unanimously that 'only those essential rights and fundamental freedoms could be guaranteed which' were 'defined and accepted after long usage by the democratic regimes'.[5]

Despite the obvious importance which it commands, freedom of movement and residence within States has not been accorded the space that it significantly deserves in the literature of international law and human rights. Much more effort has been devoted to the development of the content of freedom of movement between States,[6] perhaps because such movement, and the problems connected with it, e.g. emigration and refusal or denial of common or specified entry, are readily visible and more frequently engage the international system.

By contrast, the problems arising from the prevention of free movement and the denial of choice of residence within States have not, with the exception of the 1990s, visibly engaged the international legal domain, or the attention of international legal scholars for that matter. In reality, the problem of free movement within States has always been unresolved within the territories of States, but the growing impact of international law and human rights on domestic jurisdiction means that the protection of freedom of internal movement can no longer be treated as one of exclusive domestic reserve. However, the interested mind or speculator is confronted with the reality that the substantive content of the standards relating to freedom of movement and residence within States has not, so far, been examined systematically in international law.[7]

This book should be regarded as a tentative, although admittedly not comprehensive, effort aimed at filling this gap in the literature of international law and human rights. There is a clear need for a searching analysis of the international legal techniques for determining the legality of the denial or violation of freedom of internal movement for academics,

[4] Bossuyt, *Guide to the Travaux Preparatoires to the International Covenant on Civil and Political Rights* (Dordrecht, 1987), 253.

[5] Council of Europe, *Explanatory notes*, 218.

[6] See Hunnun, *The Right to Leave in International Law and Practice* (Dordrecht, 1981); Goodwin-Gill, *International Law and the Movement of Persons Between States* (Oxford, 1978).

[7] The existing literature includes: Higgins (as she then was; presently Judge at the International Court of Justice), 'Derogations Under Human Rights Treaties', (1976–77) *BYIL* 281; 'Liberty of Movement Within the Territory of a State: The Contribution of the Committee on Human Rights', in Dinstein (ed.) and Tabory (ass. ed.), *International Law at a Time of Perplexity* (Dordrecht, 1989), 326; 'The Right in International Law of an Individual to Enter, Stay, and Leave a Country', (1973) 3 *International Affairs* 341; Jagerskiold, 'The Freedom of Movement', in Henkin (ed.), *The International Bill of Rights: The Covenant on Civil and Political Rights* (New York, 1981), 166.

practitioners, and everyone who has a basic interest in the protection of humanity.

In doing so, a factor well worth taking note of is that a connection exists between freedom of movement between, and within, States—a state of affairs endorsed by the frequent inclusion of both rights in the same provisions and subject to the same standards of restriction.[8]

State practice appears to have long recognized the importance of both freedom of international and internal movement. It has been eloquently stated that:

> Freedom of movement, at home and abroad, is important for job and business opportunities—for cultural, political and social activities—for all the commingling which a gregarious (person) enjoys.[9]

The point which this statement underscores is that the ability to move between and within States is a prerequisite for the exercise of human rights generally. In addition, freedom of movement within States is frequently a condition for entry into the territory of States and a precondition for departure from it.[10] Arbitrary restrictions upon it can very often lead to the denial of both economic social and cultural rights including employment and civil and political rights, e.g., personal liberty, freedom of assembly and association, and ownership of property. For example, in one of its most important decisions yet, the European Court of Human Rights held, in *Loizidou v Turkey*,[11] that the violation of the applicant's right to the peaceful enjoyment of her possessions resulted from Turkey's refusal to allow her to return to her place of residence in Northern Cyprus.

The purpose of the book is to examine the standards of international law which are applicable to the right of persons to move freely and to choose where to reside within States. Emphasis is placed on the scope of protection by examining the range of restrictions which are applicable to freedom of movement within States. Throughout the book, the analysis begins from the premise of international law and assesses, in that context, the content and application of the international legal principles concerning restrictions on freedom of movement and residence within States.

The underlying justification to the approach taken in this study is commonsensical: clearly, the scope and extent of free movement and choice of a place of residence within States depends upon the nature of restrictions placed on it. Simply put, restrictions are a central aspect of the exercise of freedom of movement and residence within States. Despite considerable variation in the nature and purpose of any restrictions placed by States, the

[8] See further in Chapter 2. [9] *Aptheker v Secretary of State* (1964) 378 US 992.

[10] See Higgins, 'The Right in International Law of an Individual to Enter, Stay, and Leave a Country', n. 7 above.

[11] *Loizidou v Turkey (Merits)*, (1996) 23 E.H.R.R. 143.

standards governing their legality in international law remain the same. This means that the relevant international standards may be used to determine when and how restrictions are permissible, and when they are not; and this is irrespective of, or notwithstanding, the geographical location within which such restrictions occur.

In general, restrictions are not unique to freedom of movement and residence; they are, in truth, a constituent part of the legal structure which accommodates the protection of certain human rights on the one hand, and the protection of public security, public order, and public health, or morals, on the other hand. But the wide measure of discretion exercised by States in the choice of restrictions leaves freedom of movement potentially open to arbitrary curtailment. International law seeks to protect against this, first by prohibiting restrictions on freedom of movement in general, and secondly by providing for exceptional standards by which restrictions can be placed on the specific public interest grounds.

It has to be borne in mind that the imposition of restrictions is a function of municipal law and the categories of such restrictions are no doubt diverse. The aim is not to undertake a *comparative* study of such restrictions. The main objective of the book is to determine the scope within which restrictions are legally permissible from the standpoint of the standards of human rights in international law so that the content of the standards can be applied to a wide range of restrictions whether in Africa, Asia, China, Europe, North America, Russia, etc.

The standards concerning freedom of movement and residence within States are formulated in abstract form by virtue of the fact that they are delicately poised to strike a balance between the protection of this right, as well as the need to protect or to sustain a variety of such public interests as public security, public order, and health or morals. But the abstract nature of the standards makes it difficult to delimit the parameters within which free movement and residence within States can be protected legally. To seek to do so is the challenge which faces the present book. The writer submits that this purpose cannot be achieved by a comparative analysis of municipal practice, however valuable that may be in a different contextual framework.

Since municipal law is inevitably the source of internal restrictions, the crucial issue is to determine the scope within which internal restrictions are permissible by reference to international legal standards set by human rights. The cynic is cautioned that the problem to be confronted is neither the lack, nor the proof, of the existence of the requisite international standards, unless of course, one were to deny, or require proof of, the existence of human rights altogether in public international law.

That, in either case, is hardly necessary; the applicable standards are apparent from the sources of international law of which human rights treaties are an integral part, although one concedes that the manner of their application is not self-evident. To question the existence of international legal standards concerning freedom of movement and residence within States on grounds that the subject matter is internal or not regulated by international law is either to challenge the existence of human rights as an international legal standard applicable against the internal conduct of States, or merely to point to the unsatisfactory abstract nature of the standards in question.

While the former is retrogressive on any account of the developments of international law in relation to human rights since 1945, the latter is the more likely case and for this reason, Chapter 2 attempts to illuminate the treaty content and range of the applicable standards. The objective is to extrapolate with analysis the principles which apply to freedom of movement and residence within States. Although treaty standards obviously apply between the States parties to the respective human rights treaties, they are also evidence of State practice and thus constitute the primary basis for the existence of the applicable principles in international law.

Chapter 3 examines general restrictions used by States to regulate and control the movement and residence of persons in State territory, as well as in political unions, or economic communities. After that, the discussion turns to the legality of restrictions placed on the movement and residence of special categories, namely: minorities in Chapter 4, indigenous groups or peoples in Chapter 5, and refugees in Chapter 6.

There remains the fact that the scope of freedom of movement and residence within States is subject not only to restrictions, but also to derogations during states of national emergency. Derogations are a special type of restriction which affect the entire substance of freedom of movement and residence within States. In practice, derogations sometimes provide the means by which the compulsory movement or relocation of persons is undertaken by States. It is vital therefore to distinguish briefly the legal effect of derogations from that of restrictions on freedom of movement and residence. In effect, derogations from freedom of movement and residence may be *prima facie valid*, whereas restrictions are subject to legal justification. These issues are discussed in Chapter 7, and Chapter 8 concludes the study.

Finally, the writer reiterates that the study presented in this book is not a comprehensive treatment of varied aspects of freedom of movement within States. The ambit of the book is limited to the international legal standards applicable to freedom of movement and residence and the legality of *restrictions* on this right remains the central focus of investigation. In other words, the study is designed to be *definitive* of the standards of international law which are applicable to the question of restrictions on freedom of internal movement and residence because the writer considers this to be a very vital part of the protection of freedom of movement and residence within States.

Apart from that, the book also makes a valuable contribution to the study of the legality of restrictions in the context of human rights in international law. Within the framework of the study, the relevant standards of international law are presumed to apply within the concept of the territorial integrity of States. Therefore, the problem of freedom of movement in the context of territorial claims, the dissolution of States, armed conflict and the displacement of persons and population groups is excluded for the present moment. In terms of subject-matter, the work now presented is based on the law and material in existence as of 30 November 1998.

2

Treaty Standards on Freedom of Movement Within States

1. INTRODUCTION

It is apparent from the introductory chapter that international legal standards which give protection to freedom of movement and residence within States are evident not only in the Universal Declaration of Human Rights, but also in certain important human rights treaties. Because the treaties in question define the applicable international legal standards, and have a binding capacity on the States parties, they provide a strategic basis for the analysis of the right, or freedom of people, to move about and to choose a place of residence within States.

The aim of this chapter therefore is to identify such standards and to examine their content for the purpose of seeking to establish the framework within which freedom of movement and residence within States can be exercised lawfully. The applicable standards are identified principally from the International Covenant on Civil and Political Rights 1966[1] as well as those human rights treaties whose application is of regional scope.[2]

2. FREEDOM OF MOVEMENT UNDER THE INTERNATIONAL COVENANT ON CIVIL AND POLITICAL RIGHTS

The Covenant on Civil and Political Rights 1966 is the major standard-setting treaty which makes provision for standards relating to restrictions on the liberty of movement and residence within States. However, there are other treaties which include freedom of movement within States in specified contexts of human rights. These are: the International Convention on the Elimination of All Forms of Racial Discrimination 1965,[3] the International Convention on the Suppression and Punishment of the Crime of Apartheid 1973,[4] and the Convention Relating to Status of Refugees 1951.[5] Nevertheless, the Covenant on Civil and Political Rights is the treaty which formulates the basic standards on freedom of movement within States.

[1] For text see 999 U.N.T.S. 171; entry into force 1976. [2] See below at pp. 13–18.
[3] Article 5(d). [4] Article II(c). [5] Article 26.

Article 12(1) of the Covenant on Civil and Political Rights provides for the right to move and residence within States:

Everyone lawfully in the territory of a state shall, within that territory, have the right to liberty of movement and freedom to choose his (her) residence.

Lawful entry, or presence, in the territory of States is clearly a primary condition for the free movement and residence of persons within States.[6] Basically, the fulfilment of this condition is a mandatory entitlement to free movement and residence within States. At first sight this condition would appear most likely to affect foreign nationals. In practice, it does affect nationals as well, particularly where movement and residence is regulated by a regime of internal passes authorizing or restricting movement from one part of the country to another. The legality of such measures is considered elsewhere in this book.[7]

For the present moment, it suffices to appreciate that the use of the word 'liberty of movement' under the Covenant enhances the status attached to freedom of movement and residence within States. For liberty, in a general sense, is the right of an individual to be free from restrictions or encroachments subject only to those provided by the law and the liberty of movement referred to in Article 12(1) of the Covenant on Civil and Political Rights is an essential part of personal liberty. State practice, as evidenced in certain municipal jurisdictions, reflects this view:

There can be no doubt that freedom of movement is in the last analysis the essence of personal liberty, and just as (a person's) wealth is generally measured . . . in terms of rupees, annas and pies, one's personal liberty depends upon the extent of his (her) freedom of movement.[8]

Within the Covenant on Civil and Political Rights (Article 12(3)), the right of movement and residence within States is established as a general principle. The supposition is that persons should normally enjoy free movement and residence within States. Restrictions are permitted by way of exceptions. The *travaux preparatoires* indicate that the formula which was employed to establish a basis for restrictions in the Covenant on Civil and Political Rights sought to give protection to a person's right of free movement and choice of residence within a State while retaining adequate legal means for safeguarding State interests.[9]

To reconcile these seemingly diametrically opposed interests, Article 12(3) of the Covenant on Civil and Political Rights lays down conditions

[6] *Bolling v Sharpe* (1954) U.S. 497; *Kharak Singh v State of Uppra Desh* (1964) 1 S.C.R. 332; *Gopalani's* case (1950) S.C.R. 88 and *Kochuni's* case (1960) 3 S.C.R. 887.

[7] See further, Chapter 3.

[8] Per Justice Fazal Ali in *Gopalani's* case (1950) S.C.R. at 138.

[9] See Bossuyt, *Guide to the Travaux Preparatoires to the International Covenant on Civil and Political Rights* (Dordrecht, 1987), 252–9.

concerning restrictions which balance the scope of enjoyment of freedom of internal movement and residence on the one hand, and the protection of State interests on the other. Three broad standards may be identified, principally by reference to the obligations which set the lawful conditions for restricting freedom of movement and residence. Thus, under Article 12(3), restrictions are permissible if they are:

(a) provided for by law;
(b) necessary to protect national security, public order, public health or morals; and
(c) consistent with other rights in the International Covenant on Civil and Political Rights.

The first is a standard of general application relating to all restrictions on movement and residence in state territory. The obligation that restrictions must be provided for by law refers to the quality of the domestic law of a State party. It enshrines, in effect, the principle of legal certainty in the application of treaty obligations in the domestic law of a State party. This, however, allows subjective restrictions on freedom of movement by States.

To counter this, human rights jurisprudence requires that the meaning of the term 'laws' must be sought in the context of an international treaty rather than in the domestic law of a State party and attaches certain conditions on the quality of the domestic laws concerned. The pronouncements of the Inter-American Court[10] on Human Rights are of particular relevance in this respect. The Court gave consideration to the meaning of the word 'laws' under Article 30 of the American Convention on Human Rights 1969 with reference to restrictions on the rights in that Convention. In its view, and from the standpoint of treaty interpretation, the meaning to be attached to the word 'laws' in a treaty aimed at protecting human rights could not be disassociated from the nature and origin of certain inviolable attributes of the individual. These attributes cannot be legitimately restricted through the exercise of governmental power since they constitute individual domains beyond the reach of the State or to which the State has but limited access. Hence the use of the word 'law' is part of a set of guarantees designed to ensure that the inviolable attributes of the individual could not be impaired by discretionary acts of the State and the preliminary guarantee against this is that restrictions to basic rights can only be established by a law passed by the legislature in accordance with the constitution.[11]

[10] 'Laws' in Article 30 of the American Convention on Human Rights, Advisory Opinion OC-6/86 of 9 May 1986.

[11] Because 'such a procedure not only clothes these acts with the assent of the people through its representatives, but also allows minority groups to express their disagreement, propose different initiatives, participate in the shaping of the political will, or influence public opinion so as to prevent the majority from acting arbitrarily': 'Laws' in Article 30 of the American Convention on Human Rights, Advisory Opinion OC-6/86 of 9 May 1986 at 12.

However, there is also the inherent characteristic that the laws passed by the legislature must meet the minimum requirements for human rights in the context of liberal democracy:

> Law in a democratic state is not merely a mandate of authority cloaked with certain necessary formal elements. It denotes a content and is directed towards a specific goal. The concept of 'laws' referred to in Article 30, interpreted in the context of the Convention and in the light of its object and purpose, cannot be examined solely in terms of the principle of legality. In the spirit of the Convention, this principle must be understood as one in which general legal norms must be created by the relevant organs pursuant to the procedures established in the constitutions of each State Party, and one to which all public authorities must strictly adhere. In a democratic society, the principle of legality is inseparably linked to that of legitimacy by virtue of the international system that is the basis of the Convention as it relates to the 'effective exercise of representative democracy', which results in the popular election of legally created organs, the respect of minority participation and the furtherance of the general welfare.[12]

The European Court[13] of Human Rights has taken a somewhat essentialist approach, requiring that the law in question must be formulated with adequate precision so as to govern the conduct of persons in a State. In an often quoted paragraph, the Court stated that:

> First, the law must be adequately accessible: the citizen must be able to have an indication that is adequate in the circumstances of the legal rules applicable to a given case. Secondly, a norm cannot be regarded as a law unless it is formulated with sufficient precision to regulate his conduct: he must be able—if need be with appropriate advice—to foresee, to a degree that is reasonable in the circumstances, the consequences which a given action may entail.

The basic idea behind the American and European approaches is to ensure the positive virtues of regularity and certainty in the application of legitimate restrictions in order to avoid or exclude arbitrary restrictions.

The second applicable standard relates to the public interest grounds on which States may restrict movement and residence within their territories. Among restrictions considered as legitimate by the Human Rights Commission during the drafting of Article 12(3) of the International Covenant on Civil and Political Rights were: (a) those imposed during a national emergency; (b) for the control of epidemics, prostitution, and migrant workers; and (c) for the protection of indigenous populations.[14]

Clearly the purpose of the second standard is to limit restrictions to grounds of public security, public order, public health or morals. This serves to ensure that a State which imposes restrictions on freedom of movement

[12] Advisory Opinion OC-6/86 of 9 May 1986 at 12.
[13] *Sunday Times v United Kingdom* (1979) 2 E.H.R.R. 245.
[14] Bossuyt, *Guide*, n. 9 above, 252–9.

and residence on public interest grounds will act consistently with its treaty obligations and its action will be open to scrutiny by the international protection mechanisms. Thus while States undoubtedly have a sovereign discretion to restrict internal movement and residence on the basis of public interest grounds, human rights standards constrain this discretion in the interest of protecting human rights by providing an external basis on which justification and legality of such restrictions can be determined. In other words, the measures taken to limit the scope of movement and residence on public grounds must be proportionate to those grounds and the question of proportionality is a matter for justification and subject to scrutiny by human rights bodies.

The third standard is inherent in the requirement that restrictions on movement and residence must be consistent generally with the rights in the Covenant on Civil and Political Rights. Evidence from the preparatory work to this Covenant shows that the aim behind this standard was to provide a basis on which to determine that domestic laws restricting freedom of movement and residence would not be arbitrary.[15] This seems rather superfluous. If restrictions were effected my means of law and on specified public interest grounds, it generally follows that such restrictions would not be arbitrary.

However, to concede that a standard of this sort, occurring in a provision of a human rights convention, should be devoid of purpose or effect would be contrary to accepted rules of interpretation according to which a treaty is generally regarded as a constitutive whole.[16]

Therefore, two lines of approach are suggested with regard to the content of this standard. The first one is that restrictions placed upon a person's right to move and reside within a State ought not to negate the ability to enjoy other rights contained in the Covenant because of the interplay between those rights and freedom of movement. The views of the Human Rights Committee in *Shirin Ameeruddy-Cziffra and 19 other Mauritian Women v Mauritius*[17] tends to support this view. This case arose from immigration controls which excluded foreign husbands married to Mauritian women from entering and residing in Mauritius. Even if the case was primarily about exclusion from entry, it is relevant *mutatis mutandis* because it raised the issue of whether such exclusion was compatible with the enjoyment of other rights such as family life, equal protection of the law, and non-discrimination under the International Covenant on Civil and Political Rights.

[15] See ibid., 252–4.

[16] Dissenting Opinion of Judge Alvarez, *Reservations to the Genocide Convention* (1951) I.C.J. Reports at 52; Separate Opinion of Judge Lauterpacht, *Guardianship of Infants* case (1958) I.C.J. Rep., 1 at 89.

[17] Communication No. 35/1978 in *Selected Decisions under The Optional Protocol* (Second to Sixteenth Sessions) (New York, 1985), 70; 62 I.L.R. 390.

The Committee held that the common residence of husband and wife constituted the normal behaviour of a family, and exclusion of foreign husbands from Mauritius was an interference with the family life of the Mauritian wives and their husbands within the meaning of Article 17 of the Covenant.[18] It further stated that exclusion of residence was subject to the principle of equal treatment of the sexes which followed from obligations in the Covenant to respect and ensure the protection of rights in the Covenant without distinction of any kind under Article 2(1); to ensure the equal right of men and women in the enjoyment of all the rights under the Covenant, and also to ensure equal protection of the law in terms of Article 26 of the Covenant. By applying the third standard in the instant case, the Human Rights Committee found that there had been a violation of Articles 2(1), 3 and 17(1) of the Covenant. In addition, the Committee correctly expressed the view that the principle of non-discrimination was applicable to restrictions on all the rights contained in the Covenant:

> Whenever restrictions are placed on a right guaranteed by the law, this has to be done without discrimination . . . it is the enjoyment of rights without discrimination which must be secured.[19]

The second line of approach concerns restrictions on the movement and residence of persons within States in order to protect the rights of others. This is evident from the case of *Sandra Lovelace v Canada*[20] in which the applicant was a Maliseet Indian living in Canada. Upon marrying a non-Indian, she lost her status and right to reside in the Tobique Reserve pursuant to certain provisions of the Indian Act.

The issue was whether the denial of Sandra's right to reside on the Tobique Reserve was inconsistent with Article 27 of the Covenant on Civil and Political Rights. This provision guarantees to persons belonging to minorities the right to enjoy their own culture and language in community with other members of their group.[21] The Human Rights Committee determined that, following Article 12(1)(3) of the Covenant on Civil and Political Rights, restrictions by way of national legislation on the right of residence cannot be ruled out under Article 27 of the Covenant to preserve the identity and protect resources of certain categories of people. But statutory restrictions affecting the right to residence on a reserve of a person belonging to the minority concerned must have both a reasonable and

[18] Article 17 of the International Covenant on Civil and Political Rights provides as follows: 'No one shall be subjected to arbitrary or unlawful interference with his privacy, family, home, or correspondence, nor to unlawful attacks on his honour and reputation.'

[19] *Shirin Ameeruddy-Cziffra and 19 other Mauritian Women v Mauritius*, n. 17 above, at 70.

[20] Communication No. 22/77, *Selected Decisions under the Optional Protocol*, n. 17 above, at 84; 68 I.L.R. 17.

[21] On which see below Chapter 5.

objective justification and be consistent with the other provisions of the Covenant read as a whole. The prohibition on the right of Sandra Lovelace to reside on the Tobique reserve was unreasonable and constituted an unjustifiable denial of her rights under Article 27, read in the context of other provisions in the Covenant.

In both *Lovelace* and *Ameeruddy-Cziffra*, the Committee employed the contextual principle of treaty interpretation[22] and the views of the Committee in that regard sustain the principle that restrictions on the right of persons to move and reside within States, whether because of the protection of the rights of other persons or people, or because of specified public interests, have to be compatible with the enjoyment of the rights contained in the Covenant. It is submitted that this standard provides an additional basis for challenging the legality of restrictions on freedom of movement generally.

3. TREATIES OF REGIONAL APPLICATION

Apart from Asia, all the major regions of the world have adopted human rights treaties of regional application beginning with the European Convention for the Protection of Human Rights and Fundamental Freedoms 1950,[23] the American Convention on Human Rights 1969[24] and the African Charter of Human and Peoples' Rights 1982.[25] The standards concerning freedom of movement and residence under these treaties will now be examined.

(i) Restriction of freedom of movement and residence under the European Convention

The European Convention did not originally contain provisions on freedom of internal movement and residence when it was adopted in 1950. It was assumed, during the preparation of the Convention, that this right was an inherent component of personal liberty. Even then, it had also been

[22] See Article 31 of the Vienna Convention on the Law of Treaties 1969; Merrills, *The Development of International Law By the European Court of Human Rights* (Manchester, 1988) 72–5, 202–4.

Elias, 'The Doctrine of Inter-temporal Law', (1980) 74 *AJIL* 285; *Legal Consequences for States of the Continued Presence of South Africa in Namibia* (1971) I.C.J. at 31; *Aegean Sea* case (1978) I.C.J. at 32.

[23] 213 U.N.T.S. 221, in force 1953.

[24] In force 1978: see Organization of American States, *Basic Documents Pertaining to Human Rights in the Inter-American System* (Washington, 1996).

[25] (1982) 21 I.L.M. 59; in force 1986.

understood that freedom of movement and residence would be the subject of a subsequent Protocol to the Convention.[26]

It is not a remarkable coincidence that the Fourth Protocol to the European Convention for the Protection of Human Rights and Fundamental Freedoms was concluded in 1963.[27] Article 2(1)(3) of the Fourth Protocol to the European Convention for the Protection of Human Rights and Fundamental Freedoms embodies the same right of internal freedom of movement and residence *mutatis mutandis* as Article 12(1)(3) of the International Covenant on Civil and Political Rights. It is unnecessary to reproduce the wording since the provision in question was drafted, albeit earlier, in the mode of Article 12(1)(3) of the Covenant on Civil and Political Rights.[28] It is enough to say that, in addition to the public interest grounds on which restrictions under the Covenant may be made, the Fourth Protocol (Article 2(3)) includes those of public safety, prevention of crime, and introduces the elements of necessity and justification in a democratic society. The substance of the standards is the same however, and the epithet 'necessary in a democratic society' has the effect of enhancing the significance attached to the standard underlying the requirement that restrictions be made by law.[29]

Restrictions which are permissible on freedom of movement and residence under the European human rights system apply mainly in the context of the maintenance of public order. The incidents of lawful restrictions have arisen with respect to bankruptcy, bail, and prevention of crime.[30] In *Cyprus v Turkey*,[31] the Commission remarked that the 'alleged restrictions of movement outside the built up area of villages in the North of Cyprus would have fallen within the scope of the Fourth Protocol which had not been ratified by either Cyprus or Turkey'.

No specific requirement for restrictions to be consistent with other rights

[26] Council of Europe, *Collected Edition of the 'Travaux Preparatoires' to the European Convention for the Protection of Human Rights and Fundamental Freedoms in Europe, vol. 1* (The Hague, 1975), 222; Article 5 of the Draft Convention provided that: 'the rights enumerated in Arts. 1 and 2 (including personal liberty) . . . shall be defined in a Supplementary Agreement to be concluded subsequently between the state parties to this Convention'.

[27] The Fourth Protocol was the result of a proposal made by the Consultative Assembly in its Recommendation 234 (1960) which asked the Committee of Ministers to draw up a further protocol to the Convention to protect certain additional rights not included in the Convention itself or in the First Protocol. It entered into force in 1968. For detail see Council of Europe, *Explanatory Reports on the Second to the Fifth Protocols* (Strasbourg, 1971), 40–6; Robertson, *Human Rights in Europe* (Manchester, 1977), 1, 130.

[28] Harris, O'Boyle, Warbrick, *Law of the European Convention on Human Rights* (London, 1995), 558–62; Robertson, *Human Rights*, n. 27 above, at 130; Fawcett, *The Application of the European Convention on Human Rights*, 2nd edn (Oxford, 1987), 70.

[29] Marks, 'The European Convention on Human Rights and its Democratic Society', (1995) *BYIL* 209–38.

[30] Harris *et al.*, *Law of the European Convention*, n. 28 above, at 561; *Guzzardi v Italy* (1981) 3 E.H.R.R. 333; (1981) 61 I.L.R. 227.

[31] (1982) 4 E.H.R.R. 482.

can be found in the European Convention. However, in practice, the European Court of Human Rights has adopted this technique. In *Abdulaziz, Cables and Balkandali v United Kingdom*[32] the Court held that, even if the right of a foreigner to enter or remain in a country were not as such guaranteed by the European Convention, immigration controls had to be exercised consistently with convention obligations. The analogy is obvious: restrictions have to be applied consistently with the obligations of the Convention as a whole.

Finally, Article 2(4) of the Fourth Protocol to the European Convention on Human Rights permits restrictions on internal freedom of movement and residence in particular areas or zones. The primary requirement would be specification of the area by law and restrictions justified by reference to the purpose for which zoning is to be undertaken, e.g., country and urban planning zones.[33]

(ii) Restrictions under the American Convention on Human Rights

The American Convention[34] provides for freedom of movement and residence of persons in Article 22(1):

> Every person lawfully in the territory of a state party has the right to move about in it and to reside in it subject to the provisions of the law.

The expression 'provisions of the law' was specifically inserted in this article to confer freedom of residence exclusive of rights of established and permanent residence to non-residents[35] but it is unnecessary to belabour the import of the standard itself given that previous reference has been made to the meaning of the word 'laws' under the American Convention.

A more interesting factor is Article 32(2) of the Convention which establishes the general principle that the 'rights of each person are limited by the rights of others, by the security of all, and by the just demands of the general welfare in a democratic society'. The jurisprudence developed by the

[32] (1985) 7 E.H.R.R. 471 at 495. But note that it was the express intention of the drafters of the Fourth Protocol to exclude certain foreign nationals from securing permanent admission or residence in a State party, e.g., those who were in transit, and those lawfully present in State territory for a limited time. See Council of Europe, *Explanatory Reports on the Second to Fifth Protocols*, n. 27 above, at 41.

[33] see *Buckley v UK* (1996) 23 E.H.R.R. 10.

[34] Buergenthall Norris, *Human Rights. The Inter American System*, vol. 2, part 2, ch. 3, 'Reports on the Conference' (New York, 1982), 32.

[35] Ibid., part 2, 'The Legislative History of The American Convention on Human Rights', 161 and 32. Draft Article 20(1) had provided that: 'Every person lawfully in the territory of a state party shall have the right to move about and establish his residence in it with complete freedom'. The USA called for amendment to this draft in order to distinguish entitlement of the right between persons 'lawfully' in the territory of a State, as tourists without the right to established residence, and those with the right of permanent residence.

American system demonstrates a more radical approach to challenging restrictions. The basic proposition set by the Inter-American Court is that internal restrictions should always be employed strictly and, in order to be compatible with the Convention, they must be justified by important collective objectives which clearly outweigh the social need to guarantee the full exercise of rights guaranteed under the Convention but no more limiting than strictly necessary; the burden lies upon the State to show that a restrictive law fulfils a useful and timely purpose.[36]

The Inter-American Court has narrowed the parameters in which a State may justifiably resort to public grounds in order to limit human rights, so that a State does not have absolute discretion to decide on what measures it can adopt on the basis of 'general welfare' or 'public order'. There is a firm view within that Court that grounds of 'public order' or 'general welfare' may under no circumstances be invoked as a means of denying, impairing, or depriving a right of its true content: 'those concepts, when they are invoked as a ground for limiting human rights, must be subjected to an interpretation that is strictly limited to just demands of a democratic society' including 'the need to balance the competing interests involved and the need to preserve the object and purpose of the Convention'.[37]

A more tangible case on the legality of restrictions arose from Argentina's unpalatable treatment of female visitors to prisons. In the case of X and Y,[38] Ms X challenged routine vaginal inspections on female visitors to a prison unit after having been subjected to such inspections each time they visited their husband and father in prison. According to the prison authorities, this degrading act was aimed at combating the trafficking of drugs or narcotics in prison. The applicants subsequently refused to submit to being searched in a degrading manner and challenged the legality of vaginal inspection. As well as considering that issue,[39] the Commission examined the question whether the requirement to undergo such inspections prevented or limited the applicants from fully exercising their rights as protected under the American Convention.

In one of the most important decisions on the legality of restrictions and the protection of human rights, including those of prisoners, the Commission held that a measure which in any way affects the rights protected by

[36] *Compulsory Membership of an Association Prescribed by Law for the Practice of Journalism (Articles 13 and 29 American Convention on Human Rights)*, Advisory Opinion OC-5/85 of 13 November 1985, Ser. A No. 5.

[37] Ibid., paras. 37 and 67.

[38] Case 10.506, Report No. 38/96, *Annual Report of the Inter-American Commission on Human Rights 1996* (Washington, 1997), 50.

[39] According to the Commission, the lawfulness of a vaginal search or inspection, in a particular case, must meet a four-part test: it must be absolutely necessary to achieve the security objective in the particular case; there must not exist an alternative option; it should be determined by judicial order; and it must be carried out by an appropriate health professional. See *Report of the Commission*, n. 37 above, at 65.

the Convention should necessarily be: prescribed by law; necessary for the security of all and in accordance with the just demands of a democratic society; and its application must be strictly confined to the specific circumstances stated in Article 22 and be proportionate and reasonable in order to accomplish those objectives.[40] The relevant law of Argentina failed to meet these standards and it seems that if a measure as intrusive in the extreme as in the instant case were ever to be lawful, then very special legislation and safeguards, including the use of official and professional medical means by members of the appropriate sex should be required.

(iii) The African Charter on Human and People's Rights

The African Charter is notoriously famous for its lack of restrictions on the rights guaranteed within it. There is no evidence to show whether the underlying idea was to prohibit restrictions altogether, but the result in any case, is an ambiguous formulation by which rights are guaranteed on the condition that persons abide by the law.[41] Emmanuel Bello cogently observes that there are no defined legal reasons and conditions for invoking this limitation in the Charter, and his 'fear that this may lead to a state of anarchy in local interpretations'[42] points to the absence of a defining standard within the Charter. The standards governing freedom of movement and residence in the African Charter suffer from this defect. Article 12(1) of the Charter grants freedom of movement and residence to every individual within the borders of a State 'provided he abides by law'. The reference as to which law is imprecise and characteristically vague. If the aim was to exclude restrictions altogether, then it was short-sighted. The Charter prominently refers to peoples' rights, a category in relation to which restrictions play a large role in maintaining the balance between individual and collective rights.

Tribal Trust Lands, for example, are designated as indigenous lands where common ownership is protected by exclusive residence but there is individual ownership within such lands. In other words, restrictions are part of the menu for the protection of human rights and, moreover, States in Africa widely retain their use. If the aim behind the Charter was to insulate the domestic use of restrictions away from the prying eyes of the Com-

[40] Ibid., 62.

[41] Ramcharan, 'The Travaux Preparatoires of the African Commission on Human and People's Rights' (1992) 13 *HRLJ* 307–14, only covers background material to the African Commission. For general reading consult Ankumah, *The African Commission on Human and People's Rights* (The Hague, 1996); Kodjo, 'The African Charter on Human and People's Rights' (1990) 11 *HRLJ* 27; *Annual Activity Reports of the African Commission on Human and People's Rights* AHG/201 (XXXI).

[42] Bello, *The African Charter on Human and People's Rights: A Legal Analysis, Recueil* (1985), 70.

mission, then it was pointedly self-defeating because the very inclusion of the term 'law' within the Charter imports the application of an international standard.

This writer suggests that 'abiding by law' connotes that the 'law must' bear directly, and with precision, on freedom of movement, or any other right subject to such law; it must be legislative in character, more for reasons of certainty than any pretence to democratic values; and it must be of such a quality as to comply, or be compatible, with the obligations emanating from the standards of the African Charter as a whole.

4. CONCLUSIONS

(1) This chapter has mainly been concerned with extrapolating the international legal standards which are applicable to the right of persons to freedom of movement and residence within States.

(2) The International Covenant on Civil and Political Rights may be taken to provide evidence of the international standards which may be generally applicable to the protection of freedom of movement and residence within States. Regional human rights treaties and other instruments carrying this right provide *prima facie* evidence of the general acceptance of the standards relating to freedom of movement and residence within States.

(3) According to these standards, freedom of movement is a general right to which restrictions are the exception. Arbitrary restrictions are clearly prohibited. As exceptions, restrictions must be narrowly construed, and their legality can be determined on the basis of certain criteria, namely that they are authorized by legislation on specified grounds and that the protection of other rights is not unduly eroded by such restrictions.

3

Regulation of Movement Within States

1. INTRODUCTION

The character of freedom of movement is such that the necessity for States to regulate the physical movement and residence of persons within justifiable limitations can hardly be denied. At the same time, the manner of regulation and the basis on which such necessity is justified must be weighed against the criteria set by human rights on freedom of movement. It is a matter of public policy that a great number of States in the world today have adopted legislative or administrative measures designed to control the movement and residence of persons within their territorial bounds.[1] The purposes for which such restrictions are imposed, and the forms thereof, vary between and even within countries; much depends upon the nature and importance of the public interests which a State seeks to protect by limiting the mobility and location of persons in its territory.

Such interests may range from controlling internal migration to town and country planning,[2] monitoring the presence of persons in order to ensure the lawful presence of foreign nationals, measures of public order aimed at arresting criminality, protection of military installations, and the control of the spread of contagious diseases. This means that freedom of movement and residence may be restricted to prohibit entry into specified places and visits to certain places at certain times, or for certain purposes, and may also be restricted because of obvious danger either to the State, or to the safety or health of persons. In extreme cases, internal exile is applied whereby movement and residence is limited to particular locations—villages, towns, districts, or islands—for reasons of public order, as well as political reasons. For logistical reasons, it is impracticable to examine or consider almost every known form of restriction of movement and residence wherever it exists. This chapter is concerned mainly with the legality of selected restrictions. The focus is on the nature of specific categories of restrictions set either by municipal law, or State policy, and the chapter considers whether these fall within the range of permissibility established by international principles of human rights.

[1] For countries in which movement and residence is restricted, see Humana, *World Human Rights Guide: The Facts on Freedom and State Powers—Listed Country By Country* (London, 1983).

[2] See for example the case of *Buckley v UK* (1996) 23 E.H.R.R. 101.

The selected categories of restrictions are: the ordinary regulation of movement and residence; the control of movement and residence; restrictions giving effect to internal exile; restrictions pursued under a policy of racial discrimination; and restrictions upon the movement and residence of persons in political and economic communities. The discussion of each kind of restriction is set in a general context, with specific references being made to significant cases in point. Wherever appropriate, the content of the expressions 'public order' or '*ordre public*', 'national security', is analysed in the framework of international law generally.

2. REGULATION OF MOVEMENT AND RESIDENCE

States generally regulate the movement and residence of persons within their territory by a variety of means which include identity cards, registration, travel permits, passports or other documents. Historically, such practices seem to have been developed as a way of controlling and monitoring the presence and movement of persons within States, particularly of non-citizens.

French legislation in 1888 and 1889 provided for strict rules for the registration of all resident foreigners[3] as a way of monitoring their presence. In the United Kingdom, the first Aliens Act in 1793 made provision for the registration of non-citizens. A series of Acts continued the system of registration, notably an Act of 1826,[4] and the Aliens Restriction Act 1914[5] together with the Aliens orders made pursuant to it. The Aliens Restriction Act was passed as war-time legislation for the removal and detention of foreign spies.

The Aliens Orders made under the Aliens Restriction Act restricted the entry of aliens, limited their places of residence to specific areas and prohibited aliens from changing their residence except as prescribed by State authorities. The Aliens Order of 1953 abolished restrictions on the movement and residence of aliens,[6] but still required nationals of countries which do not belong to the Commonwealth to register with the local police.

The system of registration of persons within States spread to Africa during the colonial period. In the former territory of Northern Rhodesia, District Messengers and *Kapasus* were authorized to demand from natives at any time the production of the Identity Certificate issued to them.[7] At

[3] Haycraft, 'Aliens Legislation and the Prerogative of the Crown' (1897) 13 *LQR* 172.

[4] 7 Geo. iv, c. 54; this was later amended by an 1836 Act which continued the system.

[5] This was later amended by the Aliens Restriction (Amendment) Act 1919.

[6] In 1971 the Immigration Act repealed the pieces of legislation and orders which hitherto provided for limitation of movement and residence on the part of aliens.

[7] Native Registration Ordinance, s.16 (c. 169 of the Laws of Northern Rhodesia), and Government Notice No. 337.

present, residents and nationals are generally required to be registered and issued with registration cards upon registration.[8] In Germany, the Law on Identity Cards 1978 provides for obligatory registration in hotels, inns and boarding houses[9] for reasons of internal security aimed at restricting terrorist activities. Since May 1979, it has been compulsory under this law to fill in registration forms and to sign them as a way of monitoring the movement of dangerous criminals.

Elsewhere in Africa, Asia, Latin America, and until recently, in parts of Eastern Europe,[10] evidence of registration or proof of identity, and possession of valid travel documents are variously insisted upon as a condition for internal travel. In Zambia and Zimbabwe, local travel documents may be issued to facilitate internal travel, in addition to registration cards, to those who specifically apply. In the Sudan, the movement and residence of foreigners is closely monitored by registration.[11]

The system of registering persons does not in itself constitute a restriction of movement, but it provides a means for doing so should the necessity arise. Fawcett has observed that regulations found frequently in the national laws of the Member States of the Council of Europe requiring foreigners to be in possession of a valid passport and to register with the local police are not in any way inconsistent with the rights and freedoms guaranteed under the European Convention.[12]

A major problem however is the great potential for abuse, and the lack of safeguards against discriminatory treatment on the part of foreign nationals (from outside Europe) in hotels and police stations in Europe. In Africa, the failure to show the requisite documents either on demand such as at spot, or regular, checkpoints may entail confinement until the identity of the person concerned is ascertained and the legality of their presence and stay in the country is established. Persons who fail to produce documents in support of the legality of their presence, or to establish their identity, may be held in custody for as long as it takes to prove that they

[8] Persons above the age of 16 years must register with local authorities or the Department of National Registration. Registered persons are then issued with registration cards as proof of their registration and identity. These cards bear different colours for nationals and non-nationals.

[9] BGB 1 1978, part 1, 1712.

[10] See for example the Polish Law of 10 April 1974 on Population Records and Identity Certificates.

[11] Passport and Immigration Act 1960, s.28, requires of every alien residing in the Sudan for more than three months to apply for registration to the Registrar Officer of the area in which he resides. Upon completion of the registration, an identity certificate is issued. Under s.27, every alien shall, within three days of entry into the Sudan and of any subsequent move from one area to another, report to the nearest competent authority, and shall write a declaration concerning his identity, the purpose of his visit, the length of his residence permit, the place of ordinary residence and the date of residence.

[12] Fawcett, *The Application of the European Convention on Human Rights*, 2nd edn. (Oxford, 1987), 71.

are either citizens or residents, or that they are lawfully present within the country. Non-citizens who cannot show resident or entry permits are likely to be held in custody pending deportation. In Rwanda, the perpetrators of genocide against the minority Tutsi and moderate Hutu in 1994 relied on registration cards to determine the identity of those they sought to exterminate.[13] The system of registration tends to spawn an ideology which is inimical to the spirit and purpose of human rights. Mention should also be made of the use of electronic devices, e.g., traffic cameras and credit cards, to monitor the movement of persons which on the face of it appear to be justified in the interests of public order. There may be justification in using credit cards to trace credit card 'fraudsters' and fugitives from justice. There may also be justification in using speed cameras to detect those driving above the speed limit in order to protect the safety of other drivers. In either case, the use should be proportionate to justifiable public interest. However, two specific human rights concerns arise. One is that certain electronic devices are characteristically intrusive upon the liberty of persons in general and there is no open access to stored electronic data on the part of the public or affected individuals; the other is that there is no specific form of human rights accountability regarding the use to which electronic surveillance can be put to and the scope for abuse can be unbridled, out of proportion to specific or justified public interests.

3. CONTROL OF MOVEMENT AND RESIDENCE

Conditions of internal travel may sometimes, as shown above, require the possession of documents of identity or proof of registration, travel permits, or even passports as an essential aspect of regulated movement or residence in certain places. Where this is the case, it appears that, as a necessary corollary of the right to free movement, there is an obligation on the part of State authorities to issue the necessary documents and, where it exists, the system of monitoring the presence of persons must be regulated by human rights standards.

As far back as 1927, the Swiss Federal Court interpreted freedom of residence under the Federal Constitution to include an obligation on the part of the canton of previous residence not to impede or prevent a Swiss citizen from moving from their place of residence by refusing to provide the necessary identity papers.[14]

However, the obligation to furnish documents required for internal travel

[13] For a detailed account see Prunier, *The Rwanda Crisis: History of A Genocide* (Hurst, 1995).

[14] Bundersgericht-Sentscheid 53 (1927) i 4334 cited in Fawcett, *Application*, n. 12 above, p. 71.

also applies to non-citizens who are lawfully within State territory. But conditions of entry may specify duration of stay, and place limitations on movement and residence, as necessitated by the demands of public interest in accordance with the law. Within these limitations, non-citizens are entitled to the liberty of movement and choice of movement within a State. If movement and residence of non-citizens within such limitations is dependent on possession of travel or other documents, then there is an obligation incumbent upon the State to make these available on a non-discriminatory basis against foreign nationals.

No general right can be claimed, however, by non-citizens to enter and reside in a foreign State on a claim based on freedom of movement and residence within States. In a case where the European Commission of Human Rights entertained an application in which the applicant contested the refusal by the then West German authorities for him to re-enter German territory, and to resume his residence there, the Commission determined that no right to residence in a country of which the applicant was not a national was as such included among the rights and freedoms guaranteed by the Convention and in particular the Fourth Protocol, which contains provisions on internal freedom of movement and residence.[15]

The common reason given for monitoring the presence of persons in State territory is that of threats to public order or *ordre public*. Of course, there are legitimate interests in the implementation of criminal justice which necessitate objectively justifiable measures. But there are also xenophobic elements within States who tend to perceive a significant presence of foreign nationals on State territory as a threat to social cohesion or public order *per se*. The same attitude is apparent with respect to the presence of certain classes of persons, such as vagrants, vagabonds, and prostitutes.[16] It becomes pertinent to ask: what interests do the requirements of public order serve in the framework of human rights?

A view frequently expressed about the meaning of public order is that it denotes absence of disorder in a physical sense.[17] By comparison, a broad meaning is assigned by writers schooled in the common law system to the

[15] Admissibility of Application No. 2951/66. See Council of Europe, *Digest of Strasbourg Case Law Relating to the European Convention on Human Rights, vol. 5* (1985), 877–8.

[16] The Swedish Treatment of Vagrants Act 1885 typically defined a vagrant in s.1 as, *inter alia*, a person who, lacking means to support himself, fails to try according to his ability to earn an honest livelihood and is, in addition, leading a life that constitutes a threat to public safety, order, or morals. Those identified as such were bootleggers, swindlers, professional gamblers, stationary vagrants, i.e. pimps and professional prostitutes. Other similar cases include those persons giving no account of themselves, rogues, habitual or suspected criminals, drug traffickers, smugglers, thieves, loiterers, speculators, dealers in contraband goods, convicted prisoners, etc.

[17] Bossuyt, *Guide to the Travaux Preparatoires to the International Covenant on Civil and Political Rights* (Dordrecht, 1987), 258; Ingles, *Study of the Right of Everyone To Leave Any Country, Including His Own, And To Return To His Country*, E/CN.4/Sub.2/220; Higgins, 'The Right in International Law of an Individual to Enter, Stay and Leave a Country', (1973) 49:3 *International Affairs* 353.

French expression *ordre public* as equivalent, approximately, to public policy. However, according to French law, *ordre public* is a dynamic concept which is generally used to balance competing interests within society. It expresses positive action indispensable to the maintenance of organized society and life, including removal of threats to public peace. Thus exceptions by way of restrictions to a general rule such as freedom of movement may be permitted on the basis of *ordre public*, in order to protect a superior interest of society. In this respect, the function of *ordre public* is to permit restriction of individual liberty in the interests of society as a whole[18] provided that such restrictions are measured proportionately.

Writing in 1963,[19] the then Special Rapporteur to the Sub-Commission on the Prevention of Discrimination Against Minorities, suggested that, by inserting *ordre public* following immediately after public order in the International Covenant on Civil and Political Rights, the term public order is obviously modified in its meaning, and in interpreting it, reference to *ordre public* is inevitable. But the Special Rapporteur then went on to reject what he called the 'mischievous implications of qualifying or tying down its meaning to the French concept of *ordre public*'. He argued, for example, that if a country follows apartheid as a public policy, it would be justified in invoking *ordre public* for the purpose of curtailing the right of movement as expressed in Article 13(2) of the Universal Declaration of Human Rights on racial grounds.

These concerns are shared,[20] but they are a misplaced understanding of the French usage of the concept. In any case, subsequent developments in the law elucidating the principles concerning equal protection and non-discrimination in the context of apartheid would not justify such a view. The Convention on the Elimination of All Forms of Racial Discrimination 1965, and the one on the Suppression and Punishment of the Crime of Apartheid 1973, both carry standards which proscribe restrictions on the right of movement and residence on grounds of racial discrimination. Clearly, any previous justification for rejecting the so called 'mischievous' implications of interpreting the relations of public order to *ordre public* has been overtaken by the standards in these Conventions.

Furthermore, the jurisprudence established by international tribunals may be relied upon in interpreting the term *ordre public* or public order. In the *Guardianship of Infants*[21] case, Judge Lauterpacht explained that *ordre public* is a general principle of law covering exceptional measures of

[18] See Evans, 'Ordre Public in French Immigration Law' (1980) *Public Law* 133 and the references there cited.

[19] Ingles, *Study of the Right*, n. 17 above, 48–9.

[20] See below section 5 on restriction of movement and residence in the context of racial discrimination.

[21] (1958) I.C.J. Rep. 89–100.

protection and that it is generally used in two senses. First, it is applied as referring to specific spheres of the law, such as territorial laws, criminal laws, police laws, laws relating to national welfare, health and security. Secondly, it is resorted to as embracing, more generally, fundamental national conceptions of law, decency and morality. However, the primary point is that recourse to *ordre public* does not justify the evasion of treaty obligations in international law:

> When a state is bound by a treaty in relation to a particular subject matter it can invoke public order only if, in case its action is challenged, it is prepared to submit the legality of its action to impartial decision. It is the jurisdiction which removes the notion and recourse to *ordre public* from the orbit of uncertainty, pure discretion and arbitrariness and which endows the treaty with the character of an effective legal obligation.[22]

Certain decisions made by the European Commission for Human Rights are in agreement with this statement of the law, so that the term *ordre public* may be used independently, or inclusively of public order.

Where an applicant had been detained in prison by the German authorities and was not allowed to return to Poland, it was argued that this was a breach of the standards governing freedom of movement under Article 2(2) of the Fourth Protocol to the European Convention on Human Rights and Fundamental Freedoms.[23] The Commission upheld the refusal of the German authorities from releasing him because, in its view, the restriction was lawful on grounds of *ordre public* and that this concept covered situations resulting from the need to prevent crime, including detention ordered in the course of proceedings connected with investigations and prosecution for criminal offences. If *ordre public* justifies the taking of appropriate measures to avert criminal activity, then it also includes the maintenance of law and public order. On occasion, the notion of *ordre public* has been employed broadly in ways not limited to the criminal legal process. Thus refusal to release a person regularly detained in an institution established for the protection of the community has been held by the European Commission on Human Rights to be a lawful restriction of movement and residence on grounds of *ordre public*.[24]

The legal position is similar in the case of persons whose movement has been restricted pursuant to bankruptcy proceedings. An applicant[25] who complained that he was prevented for a month, under bankruptcy proceedings, from absenting himself without prior authorization of the bankruptcy judge contrary to his liberty, and freedom of movement and

[22] Ibid., at 100.
[23] Case No. 4256/69, cited in *Digest of Strasbourg Case Law*, at 881–2.
[24] Ibid., at 885.
[25] Cases No. 6560/74; 8988/80 in Council of Europe, *Digest of Strasbourg Case Law*, 686.

residence under the European Convention and the Fourth Protocol was unsuccessful. The Commission expressed the opinion that being forbidden to 'absent oneself' could not, as such, be regarded as deprivation of one's liberty within the meaning of Article 5(1) of the Convention. After all, this was a form of restricted liberty which left the person concerned free to come and go within the boundaries of the district in which he resided and the restriction was necessary and justified as a measure necessary for the maintenance of *ordre public* and the protection of the rights of others.

It has been suggested[26] that public order restrictions concerning movement and residence may be lawfully effected in relation to minors, paupers, persons under legal disability, fugitives from justice, persons under court restraining orders, habitual criminals, and persons whose conduct is prejudicial to orderly conduct of the internal affairs of the State. That restrictions on the movement and residence of these categories of persons are, broadly speaking, permissible on account of public order considerations is obvious, but in relation to children, the principle of the best interests of the child is paramount and overriding.[27]

The Inter-American Commission on Human Rights[28] has stressed the obligation of governments to maintain public order and ensure the personal safety of inhabitants within the territory of a State. The responsibility of States is to prevent and suppress acts of violence, even forcefully, whether committed by public officials or private individuals irrespective of political or other motives. According to the Commission, threats to public order or to the personal safety of inhabitants coming from groups making use of violence can reach such proportions that temporary suspension of the exercise of certain human rights is called for. But this must be seen in its proper context, namely that of derogation of freedom of movement during states of emergency.[29] Even so, the Commission cautions that there must be extremely serious reasons for this because the imposition of restrictions must be precisely in keeping with the measures taken to quell disturbances of public order and to ensure the safety of persons. In other words, restrictions on movement and residence must be proportionate to the necessity required to maintain order or prevent disorder. The degree of proportionality is itself not a fixed category. It must vary depending upon the necessity of the public interest sought to be protected. Restrictions which are deemed reasonable and proportionate for the maintenance of national security in times of war may be unreasonable and excessive for purposes of preventing mere disorder. Conversely, restrictions which are reasonable

26 Ingles, *Study of the Right*, n. 7 above, at 49.
27 See Article 3(1) of the Convention on the Rights of the Child 1989, U.N.Doc. A/44/26.
28 I.A.C.H.R., O.E.A./Ser. L/v/II.53, doc.21 rev. 2, 13 October 1981, 128.
29 See below Chapter 7.

and justifiable for quelling disorderly acts may be inadequate for preserving national security.

Professor Kiss[30] has argued that a definition of national security must include the two elements of the term, namely, 'national' and 'security'. From this premise, Kiss maintains that the word 'national' is generally used to refer to that which concerns the country as a whole:

> Thus, restrictions on human rights can be adopted under this concept only if the interest of the whole nation is at stake. This excludes restrictions in the sole interest of a government, regime, or power group. Limitations are not based on national security, moreover, if their only purpose is to avoid riots or other troubles, or to frustrate revolutionary movements which do not threaten the life of the whole nation. Such grounds for restriction may some times fall within the scope of public order, or public safety, but not within national security.

However, States do not, in practice, neatly categorize the nature of persons, or acts, covered by a particular public interest ground. In fact, there is sometimes an overlap in the content of public interest grounds. Measures sought to be justified under public order or public safety may well blend with those of national security. Take the following cases as examples. The *Constitution of Argentina* depicts internal disorder in terms of a foreign attack endangering the operation of the constitution.[31] In this event, the President is empowered to make a declaration of a state of siege in affected areas, and may order the arrest of persons or restrict their movement and residence by compelling them to reside in certain parts of the country. Although these measures may be taken pursuant to restoring public order, they clearly overlap with matters of national security.

Nicaragua's Law on the Maintenance of Public Order and Security 1979,[32] embodies a spectrum of matters which may fall under both public order and national security. It mentions disregard of the ceasefire in the aftermath of the overthrow of the Somoza regime, acts intended to reinstate the Somoza regime, or acts intended to submit to foreign domination, as crimes falling under public order. In its *Report on the Situation of Human Rights in the Republic of Guatemala*,[33] the Inter-American Commission on Human Rights identified political and social violence springing from armed terrorist groups as matters pertaining to the obligation of the government to maintain public order and the personal safety of inhabitants. In 1959, Greece[34] mentioned military and sanitary measures, circulation of

[30] Kiss, 'Permissible Limitations on Rights', in Henkin, *The International Bill of Rights. The Covenant on Civil and Political Rights* (New York, 1981), 296.

[31] Article 23 of the Constitution of Argentina.

[32] This legislation has been repealed in part by Decree No. 383 of 29 April 1980. The part cited here is still in effect.

[33] OEA/Ser. L/V/II.53, doc. 21 rev. 2, 13 October 1981.

[34] United Nations, *Report on Exile, Detention, and Torture* (New York, 1959), 116.

pedestrians, and traffic controls issued by the police, public danger menacing the existence of the nation, and public menace endangering the existence of the nation, as specific public order and public security matters for which it was permissible to restrict the right of movement and residence of persons within the territory of Greece.

And yet Kiss finds the explanation for the meaning of the word 'security' only in the United Nations Charter, and suggests that the term 'security' as used in the International Covenant on Civil and Political Rights corresponds to the term 'national security' as used in the Charter,[35] and concludes that 'national security' in the Covenant means the protection of territorial integrity and political independence against foreign force or threats of force.

When perceived exclusively in these terms, the term 'national security' would probably justify limitations on particular rights of individuals or groups where the restriction is necessary to meet the threat or use of external force to the exclusion of certain internal threats:

> It does not require a State of war or national emergency, but permits continuing peacetime limitations, for example, those necessary to prevent espionage or to protect military secrets.[36]

This formulation ignores the connection between internal and external security. The Argentine Constitution cited above clearly shows that threats to external security, such as war or acts of war, may lead to internal insecurity and proclamation of emergency measures. For example, the High Court of Southern Rhodesia (as it then was) held that whatever is done by the military within martial law areas in order to restore peace and order in the face of external and internal armed conflict is an act of war for purposes of Emergency Powers (Special Courts Martial: Martial Law) Regulations 1978.[37] This suggests that 'national security' may, in certain situations, involve acts of war in as much as it may involve national emergency. It is not purely by coincidence that Article 15 of the European Convention on Human Rights mentions 'war or other public emergency threatening the life of the nation' as a ground for derogation.

In terms of content, a brief survey of the relevant pieces of municipal legislation shows that the concept of national security covers a broad range of matters. It includes national defence, the safety of the public, internal and external security covering war, or acts of war, armed conflict, civil strife, acts of sabotage, subversive activities, espionage, treason, rebellion, sedition, offences against the peace or independence of a State, acts of terrorism, and

[35] Kiss, *Permissible Limitations*, n. 30 above, 297. [36] Ibid.
[37] *Deary v Acting President of Rhodesia and others* (1979) R.L.R. 200.

subversion.[38] These matters provide evidence of the content of national security as a matter of State practice. Beyond that, it is not at all possible to provide an exhaustive definition of the concept, or to offer a finite list of matters covered by it. Its meaning is relative and depends upon the context in which it is used or invoked in various States and in different circumstances.

The practice of Anglo-phonic States draws a distinction between national security and public security. Since colonial times, a good number of these States have retained public security legislation commonly referred to as the 'Preservation of Public Security Act'. Various species of this Act define public security as including defence of the territory and people, securing of the fundamental rights and freedoms of the individual, securing the safety of persons and property, and the prevention and suppression of rebellion, mutiny, violence, intimidation, disorder and crime and unlawful attempts and conspiracies to overthrow the government or constitution.[39] In this respect, public security may be seen as a 'hybrid' expression encompassing matters falling in between public order and national security. It may also include public safety, but the application of this concept may be limited strictly to a part or parts of a country, or it could be invoked in progressive stages until it covers the whole country, depending upon the demands of the situation, and in which case, national security could become involved.

So far, one can say that although the term 'public security' has a certain core, the range of the matters that it covers is 'malleable' in constitutional practice.[40] Commonwealth African constitutions permit the invocation of powers for preserving public security whenever, in the opinion of the executive, it is necessary to do so for reasons of public security. These powers broadly include restriction of movement and residence in situations connected with states of emergency of a 'preventive nature' which are clearly unjustified in international law and those restrictions on movement and residence under so-called preventive emergencies are invalid.[41]

4. INTERNAL 'EXILE'

Internal 'exile' is a form of exclusion by which persons are obliged by law to reside in a certain part of State territory and any movement outside the

[38] New Zealand Public Emergency Act 1979; Article 49 of the Statute on the Rights and Guarantees of Nicaraguans, and the Maintenance of Order and Public Security Act, Decree No. 5 of 28 August 1979; Sri Lankan Prevention of Terrorism (Temporary Provisions) Act 1979; Portuguese Act No. 2084 of 16 August 1956; El Salvador's Decree No. 507 (Annex V) 1980.

[39] e.g. Kenya Preservation of Public Security Act (c. 57); Zambia Preservation of Public Security Act (c. 106).

[40] Constitution of Kenya, s.85(1); Constitution of Zambia, Article 22(3)(b); Constitution of Zimbabwe, s.75(1)(b).

[41] See below Chapter 7.

specified area is restricted.[42] A sample of State Practice shows that in States where internal exile is practised, the purpose is to safeguard germane interests of State security and public order, including the application of criminal laws.

In Argentina, persons arrested by presidential order for subversion, or the possibility thereof, may be compelled to live in such places as may be determined in each case, with limits placed on their movement under supervised liberty.[43] The United Kingdom has a system of banishment by which the residence of persons engaged in acts of terrorism is restricted or excluded to certain parts of the United Kingdom. Under the Prevention of Terrorism (Temporary Provisions) Act 1984, such persons may be served with exclusion orders restricting their place of residence to Northern Ireland or Great Britain as the case may be.[44] The Philippines has a rather unique purpose for internal exile for the purpose of serving a penalty known as *destierro*. Crimes covered under this penalty are:[45]

(a) killing or inflicting serious physical injuries on one's spouse when caught in an act of infidelity;
(b) failure to give a bond of good behaviour when found guilty of making grave or light threats; and
(c) concubinage.

Persons sentenced to *destierro* in the Philippines are forbidden to enter places designated in the sentence, and are compelled to reside in an area of specified radius of not more than 250 miles, and not less than 25 miles.[46] And in Africa, colonial authorities and the apartheid regime in South Africa banished politically active Africans during the struggle for independence by detention or restriction of movement and residence to designated areas.[47]

The application of international legal standards to the issue of internal exile is not a straightforward matter. In particular, a borderline exists between the deprivation of personal liberty, and restrictions on the freedom of persons to move about and to choose a place of residence within States. The main point of contention is whether internal exile or banishment constitutes a deprivation of liberty, or is a mere restriction of freedom of movement and residence. This issue was the subject of the decision of the European Court of Human Rights in the case of *Guzzardi v Italy*.[48]

[42] Dissenting Opinion of Judge Fitzmaurice in *Guzzardi v Italy* (1981) 61 I.L.R. 276, at 331.
[43] Constitution of Argentina, Article 23 and Article 3 of the Institutional Act of 1 September 1977.
[44] Prevention of Terrorism (Temporary Provisions) Act 1984, s.6; see exclusion orders under the Prevention of Terrorism (Temporary Provisions) Act 1989.
[45] United Nations, Freedom from Arbitrary Arrest, Detention and Exile (New York, 1959) 184–8.
[46] Ibid., Article 87.
[47] *Ex parte Mwenya* [1960] 1 Q.B. 241.
[48] (1981) 61 I.L.R. 227; also, (1981) 3 E.H.R.R. 333.

(i) Guzzardi v Italy

The facts of the case were that on 8 February 1973, Guzzardi had been arrested and detained in Milan by Italian authorities on certain charges. Upon expiry of the detention order on 8 February 1975, the applicant was removed to the island of Asinara pursuant to the 1956 and 1965 Acts. Under the 1956 Act, persons presenting a danger to security and public morality could, subject to a prior warning by the Chief of Police, be placed under special police supervision.

Section 1 of the Act identified such persons as idlers, habitual vagrants who are fit to work, anyone who is regularly and notoriously involved in illicit dealings, and individuals who, by reason of their behaviour and style of life must be considered as habitually living, even in part, on the proceeds of crime or on the rewards of complicity therein, or whose outward conduct gives good reason to believe that they have criminal tendencies.

Special supervision in the case of particularly dangerous persons entailed an order for compulsory residence in a specified district. In terms of section 6 of the Act, a person under compulsory residence could be directed not to leave his or her home without notifying the supervisory authorities and was further required to report to them on stated days and whenever required to do so. In addition, the person concerned was issued with a card which was to be carried and shown to the police whenever so requested. The Act of 1965 extended the application of these restrictive measures to persons suspected of belonging to the Mafia. Under this legislation, the Milan Chief of Police recommended that the applicant be subjected to special supervision because he was a member of the Mafia; that he had been engaged in illegal activities, and lived off the proceeds of crime.

The applicant was compelled to reside on the island of Asinara, which lies off the north-west tip of Sardinia, measures about 200 kilometres at its greatest length and covers 50 sq.km as a whole, and is bordered by sea, roads and a cemetery. About nine-tenths of the island was occupied by a prison. Persons in compulsory residence on the island were lodged in a limited place. According to the applicant, an instruction issued by the officer in charge restricted their movement to a radius of about 800 metres, and they were required to report to the authorities twice a day. The applicant could not go out between 10 p.m. and 7 a.m. except in case of necessity, and after giving notice in due time. There was no access to the prison zone and application was to be made to visit Sardinia or the mainland if there was good reason, such as medical treatment, family grounds, or in compliance with an order of the judicial authorities.

The applicant subsequently lodged an application against the Republic of Italy, alleging that compulsory residence in a situation of virtual imprisonment violated certain rights under the European Convention. By a majority decision, the European Court of Human Rights held that there had been a deprivation of the liberty of the applicant. The Court reasoned that the right to liberty contemplated the physical liberty of the person and that its aim was to ensure that no one should be dispossessed of his liberty in an arbitrary fashion:

> In order to determine whether someone has been deprived of his liberty . . . the starting point must be his concrete situation and account must be taken of a whole range of criteria such as the type, duration, effects and manner of implementation of the measure in question.[49]

The Court thus perceived a difference between the deprivation of liberty and what it called mere restrictions on liberty of movement and residence under Article 2 of the Fourth Protocol. Apparently, this difference is a matter of degree:

> The difference between deprivation of liberty and restriction upon liberty is nonetheless merely one of degree or intensity, not one of nature or substance. Although the process of classification into one or the other of these categories sometimes proves to be no easy task in that some borderline cases are a matter of pure opinion, the Court cannot avoid making the selection upon which the applicability or inapplicability (of the right to liberty) depends.[50]

By stating that the difference between deprivation and restriction was one of degree, and that the classification of one or the other was a matter of pure opinion, it would seem that the Court was unable to find a substantive legal difference between deprivation and restriction so that the difference in application depends, ultimately, upon the circumstances of confinement. It would appear, however, that the Court's preference in applying the standard of deprivation of liberty may have been influenced by the fact that Italy was not a party to the Fourth Protocol,[51] and the provisions of that Protocol, on which the case may have otherwise been considered, could not be relied upon by the Court.

Instead, the Court confined itself to the manner in which the legislation had been applied during the time when the applicant was compelled to reside on the island of Asinara.[52] In this respect, the decision rested on the combined or accumulated effect of factors relating to the treatment of the applicant. Particular significance was attached to the relatively small size of the area available to the applicant for his movement and the fact that the applicant was subjected to supervision.[53]

The context of the case, though ignored in the decision of the Court, was highly relevant. It pertained to the dangers presented to Italy by terrorist activities and the Mafia, of which the applicant was an alleged member.

[49] (1981) 61 I.L.R. at 311. [50] Ibid., 312. [51] Ibid., 311.
[52] Ibid., 277. [53] Ibid., 312–13.

Given that the movement and residence of the applicant was restricted for this particular fact, surely the principle contained in Article 2 of the Fourth Protocol was highly relevant as a general legal standard, and it could have been applied to measure the necessity for restricting the applicant's movement and residence on public interest grounds.

Quite predictably, some dissenting opinions expressed the view that the case was one of restriction rather than deprivation of liberty. Judge Fitzmaurice, in particular, sought to distinguish between the right to liberty, and restrictions on internal movement and place of residence. He argued that the right to personal liberty under Article 5 of the Convention does not cover measures of deprivation of liberty where the basic character of those measures consisted primarily of restrictions on movement and place of residence within the State.

In his view, a view with which the writer agrees, the right to liberty guaranteed the individual against illegitimate imprisonment, or confinement so close as to amount to the same thing—in sum it protected against deprivation of liberty *stricto sensu*. But it afforded no guarantee against restrictions falling short of that, such as those on movement and choice of residence. Personal liberty must be interpreted strictly, and regarded as limited to cases of actual imprisonment, or detention close, and strict enough, approximately to a virtually complete deprivation of liberty. If this were not the case, the right to liberty would impinge on ground intended to be covered by freedom of movement and residence.

In a most persuasive remark, Judge Fitzmaurice argued that:

> It is of course obvious that all deprivation of liberty, especially if it takes the form of actual imprisonment or other close confinement, must imply restricting freedom of movement and choice of residence. It is inherently in its character to do so. But the reverse is not true. Mere exile or banishment, for instance, does not in itself involve deprivation of liberty,—or at any rate it is something that, *per se*, falls clearly on that side of the line which is occupied by the concept of restriction on movement and place of residence.

However, the learned Judge seemed to agree with the decision of the Court when he said that, between the concept of liberty and that of restriction of internal movement and residence, there may be many different degrees of circumstances and situation, so that it is always a question of where to draw the line which must in the last resort be a question of personal appreciation. Except that he indicated equally clearly that this would be in circumstances where restrictions may be accompanied by conditions that turn into a deprivation of liberty.

On the facts, Fitzmaurice was able to accept that the limitations upon the movement and place of residence of the applicant were justifiable; that the restrictive measures had been intended to put him out of circulation and not to prevent him otherwise leading a normal life. Particular significance was attached by the Judge to the general context of the case, namely that public order in Italy was currently menaced by serious threats coming essentially from political terrorism and the Mafia. The case of *Guzzardi* is a classic model of the phenomenon of internal exile, or banishment. Both the decision of the Court and Judge Fitzmaurice's dissenting views are important elaborations of the issues and content of the applicable standards.

(ii) Decisions of the Human Rights Committee on banishment

The Human Rights Committee under the Optional Protocol to the Covenant on Civil and Political Rights has stated that internal exile is a restriction of the right of movement and residence within States. In *Ngalula Mpandanjila et al. v Zaire*[54] (now called the Democratic Republic of the Congo), eight former members of parliament, and one businessman, were subjected to measures of arrest, banishment or house arrest in December 1980 on account of the publication of an open letter to the late and former Zairian President Mobutu.

On 28 June 1982, they were brought to trial before the State security court on charges of plotting to overthrow the Mobutu regime and planning the creation of a political party. After being sentenced to imprisonment and subsequently released pursuant to an amnesty decree promulgated on 21 May 1983, they were banished along with their families to different parts of the country by an administrative measure. The Committee expressed the view that the facts concerning the banishment disclosed violations of the Covenant with respect, *inter alia*, to Article 12(1) on the right of internal movement and residence, because the banished persons were deprived of their freedom of movement during long periods of administrative banishment. In typical fashion, the Committee did not elaborate upon the basis of its decision, but it accepted the allegations made by the banished persons on grounds that Zaire had failed to furnish it with any information concerning those allegations.

Some allegations raised issues connected not only with restriction of movement and residence, but also with deprivation of liberty. In a letter to the Commission, a daughter of one of the banished men alleged that the banished persons were deprived of liberty even within the locality of their banishment. She stated that a large security force had been installed all around the locality to prevent any contact with the banished persons. Inhabitants of the village were prohibited, under threat of imprisonment, from speaking to the banished persons; the customary chief of the village was

[54] Communication No. 138/1983 (1986) H.C.R. Reports, Annex viii, 121.

arrested for having allowed the villagers to communicate with the family of one of the banished persons during the first few days of their exile to the village.

Following the reasoning behind the decision of the Court in *Guzzardi*, it would seem that the degree of confinement in the instant case not only concerned the matter of restriction of movement and residence but also constituted deprivation of liberty. This aspect of the case was not considered by the Human Rights Committee. The Committee merely expressed the view that the right of movement and residence within Zaire of the persons concerned had been violated by a long period of banishment. It remains unclear as to whether the violation was due to the mere fact of banishment, or the long period thereof, or both. A similar approach by the Committee is also evident in the case of *Mpaka-Nsusu v Zaire*[55] in which the author was similarly banished to a village for political reasons. In 1977 the author presented his candidacy for the presidency of Zaire. His candidacy was rejected, and in July 1979 he was arrested and subsequently detained in the prison of the State security police without trial until January 1981. After his release, he was banished to his village of origin for an indefinite period. He fled the country in 1983 and filed his communication alleging breach of certain rights.

The Committee held the view that the long period of banishment violated the right of internal movement and residence. This view, like the previous one, lacked analytical content. Nevertheless, the views aired by the Committee in these cases are useful in showing the sort of facts according to which banishment within State territory may violate the right of movement and residence. The cases also disclose the extent to which restrictions of freedom of movement and residence are prone to abuse, and that international principles of human rights play a significant part in affording protection not only of freedom of movement, but also of other rights affected by the restriction of movement and residence. In both cases, the banished persons alleged that they had, while serving banishment, been denied medical attention and food and were ill-treated. On the strength of these allegations, the Committee found that the banished persons had suffered persecution because of their opinions, and that they had been ill-treated during banishment.

However, no reference was made by the Committee to the condition that restrictions on movement and residence had to be consistent with other rights in the Covenant, although this is implicit in its views. This criterion remains highly relevant as an additional measure against restrictions which in effect deny the enjoyment of other rights; it provides a linkage in the application of legal standards relating to the right to liberty, and those

[55] Communication No. 157/1983 (1986) H.C.R. Reports 142 at 144.

governing permissible restrictions on the right of internal movement and residence in the context of internal exile. The latter standards are concerned with mere banishment in a certain location, accompanied by a degree of liberty within bounds of the location. The former come into play when banishment is accompanied by conditions which deprive banished persons of their personal liberty in conditions approximate to detention or imprisonment.

In which event, whether banishment is valid as a mere restriction of freedom of movement and place of residence, or constitutes actual deprivation of liberty, may be determined on the basis of the criterion that conditions of banishment are consistent or inconsistent with the right to liberty. Ultimately, whatever the nature of the banishment concerned, the international standards guaranteeing against deprivation of liberty, and those concerning permissible restrictions on internal movement and residence will contend for application.

5. RESTRICTION OF MOVEMENT AND RESIDENCE UNDER APARTHEID AND RACIAL DISCRIMINATION

The system of apartheid as practised in South Africa prior to 1994 provides typical restrictions on the right of movement and residence on the basis of race. With the creation of a new South Africa in 1994, apartheid was buried, albeit decently, and all the discriminatory laws were repealed.[56] However, the abominable experience of apartheid, together with other unpalatable scourges like the genocide against the Jews in the period leading to the Second World War and against the Tutsi in 1994 must never be forgotten; the world may yet witness other forms of apartheid and genocide disguised as ethnic cleansing,[57] as in Bosnia and Kosovo in the 1990s.

Apartheid itself was a system of institutionalized racial discrimination in favour of white supremacy in South Africa. A statement made to the South African House of Assembly in 1961 by then Prime Minister Verwoerd[58] explained the abominable character of apartheid:

> We want to keep South Africa white . . . Keeping it white can only mean one thing, namely, white domination, not leadership, not guidance, but control, supremacy. If we are agreed that it is the desire of the people that the white man should be able to continue to protect himself by white domination . . . we say that it can be achieved by separate development.

[56] G.A. Res. 48/258 of 23 June 1994 on the 'Elimination of Apartheid and Establishment of a United Democratic and Non-racial South Africa'.

[57] See G.A. Res. 47/147 on the 'Situation of Human Rights in the Territory of the Former Yugoslavia'.

[58] See *ICJ Pleadings, South West Africa*, 264; see further, Judge Tanaka, Dissenting Opinion, *South West Africa* cases (Second Phase), 302–3.

Separate development was the euphemism for the application of restrictions in the movement and choice of residence of different racial groups in South Africa. Since apartheid entailed a system of restriction of movement and residence based on race, the validity of such restrictions must be examined in the light of the principle of non-discrimination. This is of equal relevance to the practice of ethnic cleansing as a denial of free movement and choice of place of residence on account of ethnic identity and by forcible means.

Standard-setting instruments in the field of human rights prescribe the general principle of non-discrimination as applicable to the enjoyment of all rights contained in those instruments. The principle of non-discrimination embodies the concept of equality. A joint dissenting opinion in the case of *Minority Schools in Albania*[59] stated that the word 'equal' implies that the right must be equal in measure to the right enjoyed by somebody else. In this way, the norm of non-discrimination enshrines the value of equal protection of human dignity under the law and it permeates the entire spectrum of the system of international protection of human rights. In the *Belgian Linguistics* (*Merits*) case,[60] the European Court underscored this point when it observed that the norm of non-discrimination under the general provisions of Article 14 of the European Convention formed an integral part of each of the Articles laying down rights and freedoms.

The Court remarked that no distinctions could be made in this respect according to the nature of these rights and freedoms, and their correlative obligations. The remarks of the Court in this case apply with equal force to every human rights instrument which has general provisions on non-discrimination underlying all the rights contained in it.

The Court noted, however, that an extensive interpretation of the norm of non-discrimination cannot be accepted, for not every inequality of treatment in the enjoyment of rights is generally discriminatory.[61] This means that although in simple terms discrimination consists in inequality of treatment of an arbitrary nature, it is important to look for criteria which enable a determination to be made as to whether or not a given difference in treatment concerning the exercise of one of the rights set forth contravenes non-discrimination.[62]

As the joint dissenting opinion in *Minority Schools in Albania* observed, equality or non-discrimination necessarily implies the existence of some extraneous criterion by reference to which the content is to be determined. Criteria for determining whether restrictions imposed on movement and residence in South Africa on account of race were discriminatory may be sought from international legal standards, the development of

[59] Per Judges Sir Cecil Hurst, Rostworowoski, and Negulesco (1935) P.C.I.J. A/B 64 at 25.
[60] (1968) 1 E.H.R.R. 252. [61] Ibid. [62] Ibid., at 25.

which has been directed primarily against Apartheid, South Africa's policy of racial discrimination.

Persistent international condemnation of apartheid[63] gave rise to substantive treaty standards concerning non-discrimination in the context of race. The most notable development in this direction has been the adoption of two Conventions by the United Nations which are specifically aimed at apartheid.

The International Convention on the Elimination of All Forms of Racial Discrimination was adopted in 1965;[64] the International Convention on the Suppression and Punishment of the Crime of Apartheid was adopted in 1973.[65] These Conventions elaborate the content of the norm of non-discrimination with particular reference to apartheid. Under Article 1 of the Convention on the Elimination of All Forms of Racial Discrimination, racial discrimination is taken to mean any distinction, exclusion, restriction or preference based on race, colour, descent, or national or ethnic origin which has the purpose or effect of nullifying or impairing the recognition, enjoyment or exercise, on an equal footing, of human rights and fundamental freedoms in the political, economic, social, cultural or any other field of public life.

Going by this provision, racial discrimination consists first of all in differential treatment accorded because of race, colour, descent, national or ethnic origin. In the second place, the effect or purpose of such differential treatment must generally be to nullify or impair equality in the recognition, enjoyment, or exercise of fundamental rights and freedoms. The International Convention on the Suppression and Punishment of the Crime of Apartheid goes further than that. It declares that apartheid is a crime against humanity, and that acts which result from the policies and practices of apartheid or racial segregation and discrimination are crimes and inhuman. The legal basis for this formulation is that acts of this nature violate international law, particularly the purposes and principles of the Charter of the United Nations, and thus constitute a serious threat to international peace and security.

Article II, paragraph c, of the International Convention on the Suppression and Punishment of the Crime of Apartheid contains a series of acts which are categorized as inhuman, and to which the term crimes of apartheid applies. These are acts committed for the purpose of establish-

[63] G.A. Resolutions: 1178(XII) of 26 November 1957; 1248(XIII) of 30 October 1958; 1375 of 17 November 1959; 1598(XV) of 13 April 1961; 2106 A(XX) of 21 December 1965; 3068(XXVIII) of 30 November 1973. S.C. Res. of 7 August 1953 declared inconsistency of policy of apartheid with principles of the United Nations Charter, and S.C. Res. of 4 December declared policies of apartheid and racial discrimination as abhorrent to the conscience of mankind.

[64] 660 U.N.T.S. 195, entry into force 4 January 1969.

[65] Annex to G.A. Res. 3068(XXVIII), entry into force 18 July 1976.

ing and maintaining domination by one racial group of persons over any other racial group, and the consequent systematic oppression of such a group.

The means by which this type of domination and suppression is effected also constitute inhuman acts and crimes. In this are included legislative and other measures which, *inter alia*, deny basic human rights and freedoms to members of a racial group. While the Convention on the Elimination of All Forms of Racial Discrimination prohibits and condemns Apartheid, the Convention on the Suppression and Punishment of the Crime of Apartheid elevates the prohibition to the category of serious threats against international peace and security, and crimes against humanity.

Group Three of the Commission on Human Rights,[66] established in accordance with Article IX of International Convention on the Suppression and Punishment of the Crime of Apartheid, found that the crime of apartheid is a form of the crime of genocide, a finding which was noted with appreciation by the General Assembly.[67]

However, in its advisory opinion in the *Legal Consequences for States of the Continued Presence of South Africa in Namibia*[68] the International Court of Justice made no reference to either of the two conventions on apartheid. In the course of examining the question presented to it by the General Assembly on the legal consequences for States following termination by the Security Council[69] of South Africa's mandate in Namibia, the Court nevertheless considered the issue of South Africa's violation of its international obligations by virtue of its practice of apartheid in the territory of Namibia.

During the proceedings before the Court, South Africa, in support of its policy of apartheid, contended that to establish a breach of its substantive international obligations, it would be necessary to prove that a particular exercise of its obligations or administrative powers was not directed in good faith towards the purpose of promoting to the utmost the well-being and progress of the inhabitants of Namibia. South Africa further claimed that no act or omission on its part would constitute a violation of its international obligations unless it was shown that such act or omission was actuated by a motive, or directed towards a purpose, other than one to promote the interests of the inhabitants of the territory.[70]

The Court found that no factual evidence was needed for the purpose of determining whether the policy of apartheid as applied by South Africa in

[66] E/CN. 4/1985/27, Sect.v.

[67] General Assembly, *Official Records: Fortieth Session, Supplement No. 53*, A/40/53; see also, *Report of the Secretary General on the Status of the International Convention on the Suppression and Punishment of the Crime of Apartheid*, A/40/606.

[68] (1971) I.C.J. 57.

[69] Security Council Resolution 276 (1970).

[70] (1971) I.C.J. 56.

Namibia was in conformity with international obligations. In the opinion of the Court, in order to determine whether the laws and decrees applied by South Africa in Namibia constitute a violation of the purposes and principles of the Charter of the United Nations, the question of intent was irrelevant.

It was undisputed that the official governmental policy pursued by South Africa in Namibia was to achieve a complete physical separation of the races and ethnic groups in separate areas within Namibia. The Court observed that the application of apartheid required restrictive measures of control which established limitations, exclusions or restrictions for the members of the indigenous population groups in respect of their participation in certain types of activities, fields of study or of training, labour or employment and also restrictions or exclusions of residence and movement in large parts of Namibia:

> To establish instead, and to enforce, distinctions, exclusions, restrictions and limitations exclusively based on grounds of race, colour, descent or national or ethnic origin which constitute a denial of fundamental rights is a flagrant violation of the purposes and principles of the United Nations Charter.[71]

The standards laid down in both the Conventions mentioned above, taken together with the Opinion of the Court in its Advisory Opinion in the *Legal Consequences* case, make it clear that restrictions based on race, colour, or ethnic origin, and which impair the enjoyment of fundamental rights and freedoms constitute discrimination,[72] contrary to international obligations concerning non-discrimination.

Among the rights included in both Conventions, and in relation to which restrictions on grounds of race are prohibited, is that of internal movement and choice of residence. The manner of restriction of movement and residence in South Africa was evident in certain repealed pieces of South African legislation. The pertinent legislation may conveniently be classified into two types. The first included legislation which facilitated the monitoring and restriction of the general movement of Africans.[73] The second type segregated residence by reference to race and, on this basis, excluded Africans from moving and residing in certain areas.[74]

The applicable method of approach in determining the validity of restric-

[71] (1971) I.C.J. 57, para. 131.

[72] Articles 2 and 5 of the International Convention on the Elimination of All Forms of Racial Discrimination, and Article II(c) of the Convention on the Suppression and Punishment of the Crime of Apartheid.

[73] Included in this category were: the Bantu (Abolition of Passes and Co-ordination of Documents) Act 1952; the Abolition of Influx Control Act 1986; Identification Act 1986; and the Population Registration Act 1950.

[74] The principal legislation in this regard was the Group Areas Act 1966.

tions placed by such legislation is illustrated by international tribunals. In particular, the approaches taken by the International Court of Justice in the *Legal Consequences* case[75], and the European Court of Human Rights in the *Belgian Linguistics* case[76] are useful. To start with, both Courts concur that where discrimination is in issue, the matter for review concerns the conformity of the relevant municipal legislation with the requirements of international standards.

Nonetheless, a difference of approach surfaces on the question of the necessity for reviewing the evidence concerning the discrimination complained of. As stated earlier, the International Court of Justice in the *Legal Consequences* case, took the view that no factual evidence was needed to determine whether application of the policy of apartheid was in conformity with international obligations. This view rested on the premise that the laws and decrees applied by South Africa were a matter of public record. The question of South Africa's intent was not relevant, after all it was undisputed that its official policy in Namibia was to achieve physical separation of the races.[77]

In contrast, the European Court in the *Belgian Linguistics* case took a slightly different approach. It stated that in attempting to find out in a given case whether or not there has been an arbitrary distinction, the Court cannot disregard those legal and factual features which characterize the life of the society in the State which has to answer for the measure in dispute.

This apparent difference of approach has much to do with the nature of the cases dealt with by both Courts and may, moreover, be perceptible only at first impression. A close analysis shows that the International Court of Justice may have adopted a similar approach in the *Legal Consequences* case. By stating that South Africa's laws and decrees in Namibia were a matter of public record, and that the policy pursued by South Africa therein was undisputedly that of separate development of the races, the Court arguably did take into account the legal and factual features which then characterized the life of society in Namibia.

The Court promptly found that these violated international legal standards. What the Court declined to do was to be drawn into the whole question of obtaining and assessing the evidence in order to establish a breach of international obligations on the part of South Africa. The racial discrimination in question was so obvious that it required no special proof. John Dugard,[78] a senior South African international lawyer, wrote that Africans were confined to their tribal homelands by a vast web of statutes, and others[79] have pointed out that:

[75] (1971) I.C.J. 57. [76] Ibid., at 35. [77] Ibid., at 57.
[78] Dugard, *Human Rights and the South African Legal Order* (New Jersey, 1978), 53–73.
[79] Brooks and Macaulay, *Civil Liberty in South Africa* (Oxford, 1958), 53.

In approaching the right of the individual to travel within South Africa it is meaningless to do so by way of examination of statutes limiting his freedom of movement, for in general the African requires some form of authority or permission for any journey of consequence within the Union. The law of the land regards him (and her) as having true freedom of movement only within the circumscribed limits of his (and her) own immediate domicile.

There is considerable support for the principle of racial equality and non-discrimination as a fundamental principle of general international law. Judge Tanaka[80] recognized it as belonging to peremptory norms of *jus cogens*, and the Court itself has said that it belongs to the category of obligations *erga omnes.*[81] This special status is not always matched with sufficient international resolve to put an end to situations which violate the norms of *jus cogens*. The lack of the political will to act lags behind the judicial will to redress discriminatory injustice.

Restrictions on internal movement and choice of residence in the context of discrimination may be manifested in an array of ways involving discrimination *in fact*, whereby a difference of treatment can be perpetuated in a way which maintains the difference in fact. Ethnic cleansing is a prime example of maintaining ethnic or racial differences by a policy of prohibiting persons of a given ethnic identity to reside in certain areas through physical restriction or by subtle means of allocating land and property.

Incidents of this character require a refined legal technique to penetrate the nature of discriminatory restrictions. The legal technique developed by the process of international adjudication to tackle discrimination inquires into the reasonableness of the objectives, the proportionality of the means employed, and the question whether a special measure involves unfairness as between one group and another. Writers have applauded this technique[82] as being applicable to cases involving discrimination only when the measure in issue either favours or discriminates against a racial group without reasonable cause.

Under this approach, the fact that a primary criterion involves reference to race does not make the rule discriminatory in law, provided that the reference to race has an objective basis and a reasonable cause. Consequently it is only when the reference to race lacks a reasonable cause and is arbitrary that the rule or practice concerned becomes discriminatory in the legal sense. Application of this technique may be seen in the general approach taken by the European Court in the *Belgian Linguists* case. The Court determined that the principle of equality of treatment is violated if the distinction or difference in treatment has no objective and reasonable

[80] *South West African* cases (2nd Phase), n. 93 below, at 208–9.

[81] *Barcelona Traction* case, (1970) I.C.J. Rep. 1, at 32.

[82] For example, Brownlie, 'The Rights of Peoples in Modern International Law', in Crawford, *The Rights of Peoples* (Oxford, 1988), 9–11; Merrills, *The Development of International Law by the European Court of Human Rights* (Manchester, 1988), 152.

justification, and that the existence of such a justification must be assessed in relation to the aim and the effects of the measure under consideration. A difference of treatment in the exercise of a right laid down in the Convention must not only pursue a legitimate aim. But that non-discrimination is also violated when it is clearly established that there is no reasonable relationship of proportionality between the means employed and the aim sought to be realized. Essentially, this legal technique is relevant for examining restrictions placed on the right of internal movement and residence not only in relation to discrimination, but also as concerns the validity of restrictions generally.

In the context of racial discrimination, Judge Tanaka[83] applied the technique as follows:

> The practice of apartheid is fundamentally unreasonable and unjust. The unreasonableness and injustice do not depend upon the intention or motive (of South Africa), namely its *mala fides*. Distinction on a legal basis is itself contrary to the principle of equality . . . and accordingly illegal.

It follows that restrictions which were placed on the movement and residence of racial groups under apartheid in South Africa were impermissible, and so are those resulting from ethnic cleansing. The ideology of apartheid is the same as that of genocide and ethnic cleansing; the difference is one of degree, not of form.

6. RESTRICTIONS ON THE FREE MOVEMENT OF PERSONS IN POLITICAL UNIONS AND ECONOMIC COMMUNITIES

The free movement of persons has gained in importance as a strategy for the pursuit of economic and development objectives in the context of regional political and economic integration in the form of political unions or communities. Policies of economic and trade liberalization and the free market have necessitated the promotion of the free movement of capital, goods and services within regional economic and political blocks (referred to as regional entities). This process began initially with the free movement of migrant workers, and it has progressively developed to include the movement of nationals as well. The major question is the extent to which the market forces and the attendant rules which necessitate free movement are compatible with the more generally applicable standards of human rights on this issue.

In strict terms, arrangements for free movement in regional communities involve movement between States. However, the difference is that the

[83] *South West African* cases (2nd Phase), n. 93 below, 314. See also at 305.

States involved agree in principle to remove internal border controls progressively between themselves with a view to establishing as a single economic or political entity while maintaining strict external border controls with other States which are not part of the regional entity. Within the regional entity—whether in the form of a Community or Union of States or both—there are often active steps taken to promote the free movement of persons, capital, goods and services. For this reason, such entities have attained prominence in constituting zones of free movement, the regimes of which cannot be set aside dogmatically. The categories of persons to which the zones of free movement apply are nationals, including migrant workers, third country nationals (i.e. nationals of States not parties to regional economic and political entities) including asylum seekers and refugees.[84]

International rules concerning the free movement of persons in regional economic and political blocks are to be found primarily in the treaty regimes establishing such entities at regional levels under organizational structures endowed with international personality in the sphere of economic and political cooperation.[85] These treaties are designed to regulate freedom of movement for economic and political reasons and they also contain grounds on which such limitations may be imposed. On the face of it, these standards must be viewed as manifestations of the legal principles relating to freedom of movement and residence in international law.[86]

Although the corpus of law which has developed (or is yet to develop in some cases) under the said treaties may acquire sophisticated expressions which characterize and enhance regional identity while providing legal techniques for dealing with regional economic integration and administrative matters, such as 'European Law', 'ECOWAS Law', or 'SADC Law', the truth is that the substantive treaty base for such subjects lies in international law and the principles of human rights equally underlie the substantive aspects of free movement. Unless this is realized fully, there is the danger that the market-oriented momentum behind the expressions will pay little regard to human rights in the pursuit of narrow economic and political objectives, and yet these and the objectives of human rights are not naturally opposed. The treaties are fully cognisant of this in their founding principles so that artificial tensions must be avoided. The Treaty of Amsterdam, for instance, professes to reinforce the importance of liberty,

[84] See further below Chapter 6.

[85] Standards elaborated by the International Labour Organisation (ILO, e.g., Article 8 of the Migration for Employment Convention 1939; Article 11 of the Migration for Employment Convention (Revised) 1949), as well as those contained in the International Convention on the Protection of the Rights of All Migrant Workers and their Families 1990, are excluded because they deal essentially with the international migration of persons between States in pursuit of employment generally.

[86] *Rutili v Minister for the Interior*, (1982) 62 I.L.R. 390.

respect for human rights and fundamental freedoms and the rule of law as the founding principles of the European Union under Article 6 of the European Union Treaty. Article 4 of the Treaty establishing the Southern African Development Community 1992[87] requires Member States to act in accordance with the principles of human rights, democracy, and the rule of law.

However, the way in which the emerging law is propagated is seemingly oblivious to the correlation between regional economic and political communities or unions, and human rights, including freedom of movement as a human right. Consequently, an artificial tension appears to have crept in between, for example, European or Community law and human rights on the issue of free movement.[88] There is the oddity that in the aftermath of the Treaty of Amsterdam, claims involving freedom of movement, immigration and asylum will be adjudicated substantially by the European Court of Justice rather than the European Court of Human Rights.

The treaties with which this section is concerned are the Treaty of Amsterdam 1997[89] which consolidates or codifies both the original European Economic Community Treaty (the EEC under the Treaty of Rome) 1948,[90] the Schengen Agreement 1985 and 1990,[91] and the Maastricht Treaty on European Union 1992;[92] the Economic Community of West African States (ECOWAS) 1975[93] as revised in 1993,[94] and the Draft Protocol on the Free Movement of Persons in the Southern African Development Community 1996 under the Southern African Development Community Treaty 1992[95] (SADC). There are other regimes of free movement not considered here, such as the Inter-Governmental Authority (IGAD) between Ethiopia, Kenya, Tanzania, and Uganda, the Caribbean Community, and the *Communuate-economique de l'Afrique de Ouest.*

(i) The Treaty of Amsterdam and the free movement of persons in the European Union

Officially, the Treaty of Amsterdam is not yet in force and the range of measures which it adopts on the free movement of persons enjoys a grace period of five years after the treaty will have come into force. In fact, the

[87] See below at p. 53.

[88] See the analysis by A. G. Toth, 'The European Union and Human Rights: The Way Forward', (1997) 34 *Common Market Law Review* 491–529; E. Szyszczak, 'Building a European Constitutional Order: Prospects for a General Non-Discrimination Standard' in A. Dashwood and S. O'Leary, *The Principle of Equal Treatment in EC Law* (London, 1997), 35–58.

[89] (1998) 37 I.L.M. 56.

[90] 261 U.N.T.S. 140.

[91] Schengen Agreement 1990, (1991) 30 I.L.M. 68.

[92] (1992) 31 I.L.M. 247.

[93] 595 U.N.T.S. 287; (1975) 14 I.L.M. 1200.

[94] Revised Treaty of the Economic Community of West African States 1993, (1996) 35 I.L.M. 660.

[95] (1993) 32 I.L.M. 120.

treaty codifies important existing treaties in force between certain European States and which currently determine the scope of the free movement of persons in the European Union: as stated before, these are the Treaty of Rome, the Maastricht Treaty on European Union, and the Schengen Agreement. The general relationship between these treaties is complex and well outside the scope of freedom of movement and residence as such. Nevertheless, it is pertinent to establish the context in which the free movement of persons has developed under the European Union and how the treaties in question affect the free movement of persons in Europe. The Treaty of Rome is the forerunner to these developments and to other regional instruments establishing the free movement and residence of migrant workers and nationals within regional entities.[96] It has normative effect in some African, Caribbean and Pacific States under the Lomé Convention 1984.

Original in character, the Treaty of Rome established an elaborate function-oriented structure under which rules governing the movement and residence of migrant workers developed with limitations justified on grounds of public policy, public security, or public health.[97] Provision was also made for the freedom of establishment of self-employed nationals of Member States, with a commitment to the progressive abolition of the freedom to provide services.[98] In relation to migrant workers, a condition for freedom of movement was actual engagement, or a serious wish to be engaged in employment in the territory of a Member State.[99]

In substance, the essential characteristic of the term 'employment' means the provision of services by employed persons for, and under the direction of, another in return for remuneration.[100] Part-time employees are included in this category, although persons in public employment are excluded by the treaty itself.[101] These provisions were augmented by important subsidiary Directives which obliged Member States to grant the right of residence in their territory to workers who were able to produce a valid identity card or passport, as well as to abolish restrictions on the movement of nationals of Member States who desired to go to other Member States for purposes of providing or receiving services.[102]

Within the original framework of the Treaty of Rome, limitations justified on grounds of public policy, public security, or public health[103] were per-

[96] There is also the European Convention on the Legal Status of Migrant Workers 1977, which came into force on 7 May 1983. However, this regulates relations between the State parties with respect to non-discrimination between nationals and non-nationals of Member States in living and working conditions. It does not as such confer rights on migrant workers.

[97] Article 48(1)(3).

[98] Articles 52 and 59.

[99] *Kempf v Staatssecretaris van Justice*, 3 June 1986, O.J. 1986 C188/3.

[100] Case 149/79, *Commission v Belgium* [1980] E.C.R. 3881.

[101] Ibid.

[102] Council Directives 68/360 and 73/48 respectively.

[103] Article 48(3) of the Treaty of Rome.

missible depending upon the personal conduct of the person concerned.[104] Circumstances in which standards concerning these limitations were applicable were the subject of the decision of the European Court of Justice in *Rutili v Minister for the Interior.*[105] In this case, the plaintiff, Rutili, was an Italian national resident in Paris. He was issued with a residence permit of the kind granted to foreigners who were nationals of other EEC states by the defendant, the French Minister for the Interior. The permit prohibited the plaintiff from residing in certain administrative areas of France, including the place of employment because the Minister believed that the plaintiff might disturb public order in those areas. Before the *Paris Tribunal Administratif*, the plaintiff argued, *inter alia*, that the restriction was contrary to the principles of the freedom of movement and residence of workers guaranteed by Article 48 of the Treaty of Rome. The *Paris Tribunal Administratif*, referred the case to the European Court of Justice for a preliminary ruling on the following two questions concerning the interpretation of Article 48:

(a) Does the expression, subject to limitations justified on grounds of public policy, employed in Article 48 of the Treaty establishing the EEC concern merely the legislative decisions which each Member State of the EEC has decided to take in order to limit within its territory the freedom of movement and residence for nationals of other Member States or does it also concern individual decisions taken in application of such legislative decisions?

(b) What is the precise meaning to be attributed to the word 'justified'?

On the first question, the Court held that the provisions of Article 48 regarding permissible restrictions on the free movement of persons were applicable not only to legislative provisions of the Member States but also to individual decisions taken pursuant to such legislation.

In holding thus, the Court underscored the necessity for relevant domestic legislation to be compatible with standards set by Community law.[106] Therefore, the requirement in Directive 64/221, that restrictive measures be based exclusively upon the personal conduct of the person concerned, also pointed to the application of Community law to each decision.

On the second question, the Court decided that the term 'justified' in

[104] Council Directive 64/221, Article 3. See also, *Carmelo Angelo Bonsingnore*, Case 67/74 [1975] E.C.R. 279 at 307; *Van Duyn v Home Office* [1974] E.C.R. 1337; *Adoui and Cornuavaille v Belgium* [1982] E.C.R. 1665.

[105] (1982) 62 I.L.R. 390.

[106] The Court stated that the relevant provisions of Community law conferred rights directly upon nationals of Member States, so that it was important that national courts, as well as giving precedence to those provisions over national legislation, exercised judicial review of decisions in individual cases to ensure that they complied with Community law.

Article 48(3) meant that only limitations which complied with Community law, as well as national law, were permissible. On this view, the rules of Community law on free movement were simply a specific manifestation of the general principles enshrined in the European Convention on Human Rights with a call for a strict interpretation of the concept of public policy corresponding to a human rights standard. Since the provisions of Article 2 of the Fourth Protocol to the European Convention on Human Rights reflect general international legal standards relating to restrictions on freedom of internal movement, it follows that a strict interpretation of a restrictive public policy is generally desirable.

In *Rutili*, the Court ruled that restrictions on the movement of a national of another Member State should be imposed only if their presence or conduct constituted a serious threat to public order and not to service economic ends, or to restrict the exercise of trade union rights. This statement, together with the requirement in Directive 64/221, would seem to rule out restrictions based on general considerations unrelated to the conduct of the person concerned.

If restrictions were to be imposed on account of general considerations, then such restrictions would inevitably have to apply generally. The Court made it explicit that prohibitions on residence under Article 48(3) of the Treaty of Rome had to apply to the whole territory of the State concerned on a non-discriminatory basis between nationals of Member States.[107] Thus, a State could only prohibit a national of another Member State of the EEC from residing in a particular area in circumstances in which it could impose a similar prohibition on one of its own nationals. Procedural safeguards must also apply to limitations on movement. The Court required of such limitations to comply with the individual's right to be heard and to be informed of the grounds on which their movement was being (or proposed to be) restricted, unless this would endanger the security of the State.

However, the latter may be at odds with guarantees of procedural fairness and the right to a fair hearing which, under Art 6, of the European Convention, is not subject to restrictions or derogation in the public interest.

The scope of free movement has expanded considerably with the establishment of the European Union under the Treaty on European Union (the Maastricht Treaty) in 1992. This process began with the adoption of the Single European Act in 1986 by ten Member States of the European Community who launched the idea of 'Europe 1992'. The aim of this was to introduce a new provision (Article 8A) into the Treaty of Rome[108] with the objective of progressively establishing an internal market over a period expiring on 31 December 1992.

However, earlier in 1985, a parallel process had begun, spearheaded by

[107] Article 48(2) of the Treaty of Rome.
[108] By virtue of Article 13 of the Single European Act, (1986) I.L.M. 206.

Germany and France, and joined by the Benelux countries in what became known as the Schengen Agreement 1985 gradually to abolish checks at common borders. The Schengen Agreement entered into force in 1990 while the 'Europe 1992' process was introduced by the Maastricht Treaty in 1992. The Maastricht Treaty legally asserts the principle of the removal of internal frontier controls and regulates the three pillars of the Common Market (first pillar), the Common Foreign and Security Policy (second pillar), and the Common Justice and Home Affairs (third pillar).

The Treaty of Amsterdam maintains this three pillar structure but makes certain important changes. It establishes, within the first pillar, new provisions on visas, asylum, and immigration policies concerning third-country nationals and refugees alongside the free movement of persons in the European Community and Union. In addition, the Schengen Agreement on the gradual abolition of internal border controls is integrated formally in the framework of the European Union by means of Protocol 2 so that the Schengen States system is effectively a part of the regime of the European Union. However, Protocols 3, 4, and 5 exempt the United Kingdom, Ireland and Denmark from the regime governing the free movement of persons in the European Union and there is special recognition for the existence of the Common Travel Area between the United Kingdom and Ireland.

Pointedly, the original EEC arrangements on internal market freedoms fall under the first pillar, including matters of agriculture, competition policy, economic and monetary policy, common commercial policy, social policy, consumer protection, the environment and culture, and the institutions of the European Parliament, the Council, Commission, Court of Justice and Court of Auditors. Common and Foreign Policy has remained under the second pillar in the Amsterdam Treaty, but the third pillar (Justice and Home Affairs) has been recast 'Police and Judicial Cooperation in Criminal Matters' with a view to strengthening police and judicial cooperation in criminal matters.

In so far as free movement is concerned, the objective of the Treaty of Amsterdam is to ensure the free movement of persons throughout the European Union within five years after entry into force. Under the treaty, Citizenship of the Union[109] entails freedom of movement for nationals of Member States within the European Union generally and subject to certain limitations of public policy. Notably, the special protection accorded to the movement of workers within the EEC is retained by Article 39 of the Treaty of Amsterdam which incorporates the original provisions of Article 48 of the Treaty of Rome.[110] The basic form of protection of the movement of workers is the commitment to the abolition of any discrimination between workers of Member States by reference to their nationality where employment, remuneration and other conditions of employment are concerned.

[109] Articles 17–22 of the Treaty of Amsterdam, with Articles 17 and 18 codifying Articles 8 and 8A of the Treaty of Rome.

[110] See above at pp. 46–8.

In practice, the right to accept offers of employment actually made is based on the freedom to move and to remain within the territories of Member States for the purpose of employment. Under Article 39, such freedom of movement is subject to limitations justified on grounds of public policy, public security or public health and the decision of the European Court of Justice in *Rutili* applies to these provisions.[111] However, freedom of movement in pursuit of the right of establishment, i.e. the right of nationals of Member States to take up and pursue activities as self-employed persons who may set up and manage undertakings, particularly in companies or business firms, receives stronger protection by virtue of the exclusion of any restrictions on it.[112]

A more problematic issue concerns the movement of third country nationals, i.e., persons not citizens of the European Union or its Member States. The Amsterdam Treaty provides a legal framework for the imposition of conditions which will determine external entry, stay and free movement within the Union. These include the following.

(a) Member States are to prescribe standards and procedures for carrying out checks on persons when crossing external borders. Article 63(3) in particular envisages the adoption of immigration measures setting conditions of entry and residence as well as standards on procedures for the issue by Member States of long-term visas and residence permits for the purpose of family reunion. It is worth noting that this measure is not subject to the five-year grace period after the entry into force of the Treaty of Amsterdam. A stated objective to be achieved in tandem with establishing strict immigration controls is to combat illegal immigration by repatriating illegal immigrants to States of origin. One way in which this is being done is by concluding readmission agreements, both bilateral and multilateral, concerning the return of third-country nationals residing illegally in the European Union to the contracting States to which the nationals belong. Another way, taken by France, is to regularize the status of given categories of illegal immigrants as a unilateral act.

(b) Rules are to be adopted on visas for intended stays of no more than three months, listing third countries whose nationals must be in possession of visas when crossing external borders and those whose nationals are exempt from this requirement. The latter clearly accommodates bilateral or reciprocal arrangements waiving visa requirements between Member States and States outside the European Union, but it is by no means clear, let alone possible, that nationals of the latter will gain unrestricted entry into the territories of other European Union Member States on the strength of these arrangements.

(c) General procedures and conditions for issuing visas by Member

[111] See below at pp. 46–8.

[112] Article 43 of the Treaty of Amsterdam which codifies Article 52 of the Treaty of Rome.

States are to be set up, as well as rules on uniform format visas. The aim, presumably, is first to harmonize the conditions and procedures for issuing visas to third-country nationals, and secondly, to adopt uniform visas and formats. An example of a uniform visa is the Schengen visa which, if issued by any Schengen Member State will permit a third-country national holder to enter the territory of any Schengen State provided that the visa is a valid one and the entry is made within the stipulated period. This advantage, leaving aside the conditions of issuance, would clearly benefit third-country nationals in possession of uniform visas for the European Union.

The dichotomy between uniform and 'other visas' between Member States of the European Union has a detrimental effect on freedom of movement which is exemplified by the uniform Schengen visa on the one hand, and non-uniform visas on the other hand. Between the Schengen States—take the Netherlands and Germany in this case—International Airports such as Schipol in Amsterdam (Netherlands) and Frankfurt (Germany), are internally divided into Schengen and non-Schengen territory for the purpose of international movement. X, a third-country national with a visa issued by the United Kingdom (a non-Schengen State Member), must obtain a Schengen visa to cross over the non-Schengen part of Schipol airport to the Schengen part of the same airport in order to get to a connecting flight to Frankfurt and will meet the same predicament to fly out of Frankfurt to, say Ethiopia.

(d) Member States are to introduce measures defining the rights and conditions under which nationals of third countries legally resident in a Member State of the European Union may reside in other Member States. Ideally, such measures will solve the problem depicted above by entailing freedom of movement within the European Union for third-country nationals, except—it seems—for those residing in States such as the United Kingdom, Ireland and Denmark which have opted out of the free movement regime. These measures are not subject to the five-year grace period after the entry of the Treaty of Amsterdam.

However, there seems to be a lack of consensus within the European Union on how to proceed on this issue. There are proposed Directives seeking to give effect to the Maastricht process awaiting adoption by the Council of Europe. The first, a 'catch-all', seeks to implement the abolition of internal controls at internal frontiers and spell out the formalities for this process in general. The second, which has been greeted with controversy, concerns the right of third-country nationals with residence permits or visas to move freely to other Member States for short periods, and the third is intended to amend existing Directives[113] which require proof of identity on the part of migrant workers and nationals.

[113] These are Directives 68/360 and 73/148.

(ii) The Economic Community of West African Communities

The model set by the Treaty of Rome regarding the free movement of persons was adopted by ECOWAS in West Africa[114] in 1975. However, the original treaty has now been revised in the light of the creation of the African Development Community 1991[115] which advocates regional economic integration as a development strategy and casts the free movement of persons as an important part of this strategy, while recognizing that free movement between African States is an historical phenomenon crudely curtailed by the advent of State boundaries set during colonialism.

To begin with, the preamble to the original treaty of ECOWAS recognized the need for the removal of obstacles to the free movement of goods, capital and persons within the West African Community, and Article 27 of the Treaty provided for the free movement of persons within this Community. It also established the status of Community citizenship to the citizens of Member States, and obliged the States parties to undertake to abolish, within the Community, obstacles to the free movement and residence of citizens. But questions of exempting Community citizens from holding visitors' visas and residence permits, and of allowing them to work in the territories of Member States, were left open to be negotiated for in separate agreements between Member States. The revised Treaty departs from this formula and its provisions are less charitable than those of the original treaty. Under Article 59, citizens of the Community shall have only the right of entry, residence and establishment, and the Member States only undertake: to recognize these as rights of Community citizens in accordance with the provisions of the relevant Protocols; to adopt all appropriate measures to ensure that Community citizens enjoy the stated rights fully; and to adopt all the necessary measures at national level to give effective implementation of the rights concerned.

The reference to the Protocols obviously includes the Protocol concluded on 29 May 1979 pursuant to the provisions of the original treaty (Article 27). However, it is unclear whether that Protocol will altogether be open for negotiation in the light of the new Treaty, but all indications are that it is still in force. It sets out three phases of five years each in which the principle of free movement of migrant workers was to be realized progressively, beginning from June 1980. The phases were respectively aimed at achieving the guaranteed right of entry of Community citizens without the

[114] The Parties to the Treaty of ECOWAS are: Benin, Burkina Faso, Cape Verde, Gambia, Guinea, Guinea-Bissau, Ivory Coast, Liberia, Mali, Mauritania, Niger, Senegal, Sierra Leone, and Togo. The Member States of CEAO are: Burkina Faso, Ivory Coast, Mali, Mauritania, Niger, and Senegal.

[115] (1991) A.L.M. 3. Others include the Treaty establishing the Southern African Development Community 1992, (1993) 32 I.L.M. 116 under which free movement is the subject of a draft protocol of 15 March 1996; Treaty for the establishment of the Economic Community of Central African States 1983, (1984) 23 I.L.M. 945.

requirement for visas, securing the right of residence within the territories of Member States, and conferring the right of establishment. The terms of the Protocol appear to be more in tune with the revised Treaty, but neither the Treaty nor the Protocol carry any standards pertaining to the grounds upon which free movement and residence within the Community may be restricted. Instead, the Protocol carries a general provision reserving the right of Member States to refuse admission to any citizen who, according to local law, comes within the category of an inadmissible immigrant.

The reference to local law left a potentially exploitable loophole by Member States in furtherance of their individual interests. Each Member State retained a discretion unfettered by the Treaty, unilaterally to exclude or restrict entry, movement and residence, or expel migrant workers in accordance with its domestic law, without external Community supervision. Consequently, when the second phase of the said Protocol commenced on 4 June 1985, Nigeria declared that it would unilaterally impose conditions regarding the implementation of this phase. Conditions set by Nigeria allowed unrestricted entry into its territory only to persons belonging to certain professions, i.e. engineers, surveyors, teachers and bilingual secretaries. These were to be permitted to reside in Nigeria provided that they secured employment in a limited period of six months.

This episode demonstrates that collective approaches to free movement on regional basis must sufficiently curtail unilateral action which may be triggered by national or local difficulties. It is those States which are powerfully dominant in economic and political terms within regional communities that are likely to act unilaterally and the best strategy is to set criteria and agreement for opting-out on a pre-determined basis by reference to structural economic and social and geographical considerations.

(iii) Free movement in the Southern African Development Community

Historical relics to the institutionalized movement of persons in Southern Africa lie partly in the ill-fated Central African Federation (defunct in 1963) and partly, in the system of migrant workers from Lesotho, Mozambique, Swaziland, Zambia and Zimbabwe to South African mines during and after apartheid. It was thus inevitable that a new, post-apartheid South Africa would bear the brunt of migration from within and outside Southern Africa.

Given this background, it is surprising that the issue of the free movement of persons was not addressed directly in the original treaty which established the Southern African Development Community in 1992.[116]

[116] SADC was established originally as the Southern African Development Coordinating Conference in 1980 with the aim of achieving integrated economic development and bolstering the economic and political independence of the then participating States against apartheid South Africa. The current members of SADC are: Angola, Zimbabwe, Democratic Republic of the Congo, Lesotho, Malawi, Mozambique, Namibia, South Africa, Swaziland, Tanzania, Zambia and Zimbabwe.

Priority was given first to laying the legal foundations for establishing the Community in order for it to develop policies aimed at the progressive elimination of obstacles to the free movement of capital and labour, goods and services, and of people belonging to the region in general. However, as the tide of unbridled, often speculative, movement towards the new South Africa grew alongside the pre-existing migrant labour system, it became clear that a collective regional approach to free movement in Southern Africa was desirable.

In addition to this, the impetus to establish a regime for the free movement of persons in SADC grew from the demand for creating a regional economic market for the free movement of goods and services. Hence the Protocol on the Free Movement of Persons in the Southern African Development Community (SADC) was drafted in 1996 and adopted in 1998 to provide the legal basis for facilitating the free movement of persons as a vehicle for achieving economic and social development through the economic integration of the SADC States.[117]

The Protocol is not yet in force and it is unlikely to be so in the near future because the range of obligations which it establishes require harmonization of the Member States' laws and related practices in the fields of immigration and refugees, including the abolition (or free issuance) of visas, the introduction of 'border passes' and a uniform SADC passport for use within SADC and such other third States as may be agreed.[118] These will take time to put in place but they are not in themselves obstacles to the entry into force of the Protocol as such.

Officially the projection is that the Protocol will enter into force 30 days after the deposit of the instruments of ratification by two-thirds of the Member States. It follows that a real test to the commitment of the SADC States towards free movement will lie in the speed by which the Protocol will be ratified, let alone be implemented, and this, in turn, will depend upon the level of economic pressures and political will to realize the Protocol's underlying objectives. The Preamble to the Protocol extols free movement as a means of promoting popular participation in the transformation or development of the Southern African region into a Community for the free movement of goods, services, and of the citizens of that Community.

The approach to establishing the right of persons to move freely within the SADC States is cautious. Three types or segments of free movement are envisaged, namely: the right of 'visa-free' entry; the right of 'residence';

[117] See Article 10(2) of the Protocol on the Free Movement of Persons in SADC; Article 10(3) of the SADC Treaty authorizes SADC to adopt legal instruments for the implementation of the Treaty.

[118] See Chapter V, Article 14 of the Protocol on the Free Movement of Persons in the Southern African Development Community 1998.

and the right of 'establishment'. Within the Protocol, the principle of progressive implementation has been employed so that each of these forms of free movement is set to be achieved over four graduated phases of varying lengths to run concurrently.[119]

The first implementation phase will aim to bring about visa-free entry which, by definition, will be available on short visits of not more than six months' duration. Basically, 'visa-free entry' is the simplest and most obvious form and basis of free movement designed by SADC. This is a right of entry which connotes a duty of admission on the part of SADC States without the requirement of a visa. But an applicant for 'visa-free admission' must meet the condition that the visit does not exceed six months, subject to extension on application to the host State,[120] and that the visitor must be in possession of a valid travel document, is not a prohibited immigrant, and obtains entry at an officially designated border post. The latter may seem obvious enough, but the point of making regular entry a condition for free movement has to be appreciated in light of the need to combat irregular entry and movement (with the exception of refugees) because of long and open land boundaries between the States involved.

The scope of 'visa-free admission' as a basis for the right to free movement within SADC extends to any vehicle which is registered in the territory of a Member State and is used for the transportation of persons whether for personal, private or commercial purposes; such vehicles may remain within the territory of a Member State for a period not exceeding six months. However, the question of the treatment of goods brought into the territories of Member States by nationals of other Member States remains contentious and the Protocol establishes only a duty on the part of Member States to cooperate closely to harmonize their laws in respect of such goods. Equally contentious is the problem of the treatment of commercial goods, which has been deferred to the process of elaborating another Protocol on Trade.[121]

There does not appear, in the Protocol as a whole, to be any defined basis for permitting restrictions on the right of entry on public grounds permitted by human rights standards. It seems that the remedy in lieu of restrictions on entry is one of exemption by the Summit of the Member States, and the requesting State is obliged to furnish the Summit with a written notice and to show good reason for seeking exemption from its obligations to admit SADC nationals.[122] Conditions for such exemption are defined stringently, both in duration and substance, with a view to ensuring that exemption should not provide a recourse for contracting out of the obligations of the Protocol. Thus the exemption can only be valid for a period not

[119] Ibid., Chapter III, Article 5. [120] Ibid., Chapter VI, Article 15.
[121] Ibid., Article 18. [122] Ibid., Article 16.

longer than 12 months and it permits a Member State to impose entry visas on SADC nationals on the condition that such nationals will be able to obtain them at the point of entry at the border and that no fee shall be levied in respect of such visas.

The concept of exemption may be related to that of restrictions which are permitted by human rights standards and in showing 'good reason' for seeking exemption from the regime of free movement under SADC, a Member State may advance certain public interest grounds with justification. For example, in the face of civil strife, both Angola and the Democratic Republic of the Congo may invoke public security, while South Africa may invoke public order because of the high rate of criminality in that country. Provided that economic factors *per se* are not grounds for negating the free movement of persons; the conditions set by the Protocol with regard to the exemption of Member States have to be viewed in that perspective and they are a vast improvement to the ECOWAS model which grants individual Member States a measure of discretion on this point.

The right of residence occupies the second phase of the implementation of the regime of free movement in SADC, to come into effect within three years from the entry into force of the Protocol. Article 20 of the Protocol establishes an obligation for Member States to grant SADC nationals the right of residence within their territories regardless of whether this implies seeking employment or engaging in other income-generating activities. For non-citizens residence permits are the mode through which the right of residence is normally obtained, and for this reason a special duty exists in Article 21(4) to harmonize Member States' laws and regulations concerning the grant of residence permits as well as to establish a uniform SADC residence within a period of two years from the entry of the Protocol. In any case, to assert a right of residence within a treaty framework suggests that there is a duty to issue such permits as a matter of treaty obligations. Ideally, the process of harmonization should see to that. But the dividing line between the obligation to issue a residence permit, and the discretion which States usually enjoy in such matters remains unclear.

The content of the right of residence within SADC is similar to the EEC model and the pertinent elements are as follows (Article 19):

(a) to live in the territory of a Member State in accordance with its legislative and administrative provisions. However, the duration of this right is limited and the Protocol specifies a residence permit for a maximum period of three years. Clearly, the quality of the legislative and administrative provisions involved should be compatible with the Treaty through the process of harmonization, but this can by no means be ascertained;

(b) to apply for and accept the offer of employment where actually made. This, too, is subject to a maximum period of three years' residence;
(c) to enter freely the territory of a Member State for the purpose of seeking employment, also subject to three years' maximum residence;
(d) to reside in the territory of a Member State in order to take up employment subject to the labour laws of the Member State. No limitation applies here and the duration of residence is determined by the contract of employment;
(e) to reside in the territory of another Member State as a student or trainee for a period equivalent to the length of the period of study of training required by the applicant.

The three-year maximum residence rule is subject to the qualification that residence permits are subject to renewal. The explanation for it would appear to be that residential status under immigration rules in the SADC States often changes after three years of continuous employment.

The right of establishment marks a decisive stage in the implementation of freedom of movement within SADC.[123] Within five years from the entry into force of the Protocol, each Member State is obliged to grant to SADC nationals resident in its territory the right of establishment and this entails the progressive abolition of all restrictions on the freedom of establishment in respect of such nationals (Article 26). Consequently, new restrictions on freedom of establishment after the entry into force of the Protocol are expressly forbidden in Article 28 of the Protocol.

The substantive content of the right of establishment under the SADC Protocol is derived from the EEC design. In principle this is about 'establishing' oneself with a pre-eminent degree of self-reliance in the territory of a Member State. It includes the right of self-employed persons to reside in the territories of Member States and to have access to economic activities; the right to establish and manage a profession, trade or business; the right to practise one's profession, trade, business or calling and to provide related services; and the right to participate in all activities to the same extent as the nationals of a host or Member State, except where political activities are concerned. But special provision is made for employed persons to 'convert' salaried employment into establishing themselves by means of 'unsalaried' economic activity at the conclusion of their salaried employment.

Both the right of residence and the right of establishment are subject to

[123] See Chapter V, Article 14 of the Protocol on the Free Movement of Persons in the Southern African Development Community 1998. Chapter VIII, Article 25.

special protection (Articles 29–30) on the basis of equal treatment, or non-discrimination, with respect to human rights and freedoms enjoyed by nationals of a Member State, except, as noted above, in the sphere of political activity. Additional protection (Article 29(2)) is accorded to the right of establishment in connection with fair and equitable treatment in matters of capital investment, the prohibition on confiscation or expropriation of property, except where nationals of a Member State are subject to the same treatment legally. The principle of equal treatment applies with regard to all living conditions, including security of employment and employment benefits, access to health and recreational facilities, access to education, training facilities and professional advancement, and in the enjoyment of freedom of association, i.e. the right to belong to trade unions.

Injunctive measures have been drafted against the repatriation and expulsion (both individual and mass) of persons who hold rights of establishment and residence, apart from where national security is threatened or where residence or establishment permits are no longer valid (Articles 31–34). The Member States clearly regard repatriation or expulsion of SADC 'nationals to be "a serious matter having a potential effect on inter-State relationships" within the SADC community' (Article 35).

The final phase establishing a free movement regime in SADC involves the abolition of entry controls at internal borders while maintaining those at external borders as in the case of the European Union (Article 36). Although the Protocol fails to address this issue, the supposition is that the short-term 'non-visa' right of entry will have become redundant after the coming into effect of this phase. This is projected somewhat vaguely to take place within a period of ten years, presumably after the Protocol will have entered into force (Article 36) but the date of entry of this part of the Protocol will fall to be determined by the Summit of the Heads of State of SADC (Article 44).

However, each Member State retains a discretion in the way in which it will monitor the movement of persons within its territory. The Protocol does allude to the right of Member States to require persons to carry and produce permits and identity documents under their respective laws (Article 36 (4)). There is a strong guarantee of freedom of movement limited only by the fact that movement across internal borders may be suspended by a Member State for not longer than one month in the interests of public order, public health or national security (Article 37) provided that due notice is given and application is made by the State in question to the Summit of the Heads of State of SADC. In essence, a suspension of freedom of movement on these grounds invokes the application of restrictions on freedom of movement with the consequence that the analysis presented in Chapter 2 is applicable here.

A refreshing factor is that the treatment of third-country nationals under the Southern African Development Community is infinitely better and straightforward. Although, clearly, the projected abolition of internal checks on SADC nationals does not affect any rights or obligations of third-State nationals, and while a common policy is to be agreed in the long term on the question of visas for non-SADC nationals, nevertheless Article 34 carries the categorical commitment that 'The admission of any person who is a citizen of a Third State into the territory of a Member State under this Protocol shall entitle such person to enter and travel freely in the territories of other Member States for a period not exceeding three months.' The fact that there is a forecast legal commitment to develop agreements with third States or communities of third States to secure the reciprocal treatment of the nationals of Member States resident in such third States or communities means that the Southern Africa Development Community has a potential leverage for putting in place measures concerning free movement which may lead to better or worse treatment for its nationals abroad, or at least to treatment as good, or as bad, as it is capable of reciprocating in matters of free movement.

7. CONCLUSIONS

(1) The movement and residence of persons within State territory is ordinarily subject to regulation by the State. Forms of regulation vary in time and place. The registration of persons is commonly employed to monitor the presence or movement of certain categories of persons within States. Strictly speaking, registration of itself is not a restriction or limitation of movement and residence, but much depends on the purpose and justification for it. The practice is prone to abuse and it is susceptible of manipulation for invidious motives contrary to the spirit of human rights.

(2) However, when evidence of registration in the form of identity cards, or other documents, is required as a condition for internal movement and residence, registration becomes a form of control of movement and residence. In this sense, registration may be an indirect restriction of internal movement and residence. There is a duty not to constrain freedom of movement by bureaucratic means and this duty includes the provision of such documents in order to facilitate internal movement.

(3) Restrictions imposed due to public interest grounds may be based on general considerations, or may apply to individual persons. In the former, restrictions must apply generally, as a matter of public policy, and without discrimination. In the latter case, restrictions must be based on the actual conduct of the person in relation to a specified public interest. There must be proof of actual involvement threatening such an interest on the part of the person concerned, and reasons for the restriction must be specified.

(4) Standards pertaining to the movement and residence of persons in regional entities have amplified the scope of and content of free movement to the extent that they may be regarded as 'zones' or 'regimes' of free movement. These show that human rights standards on freedom of movement are compatible with the free movement of persons engineered as a special feature of the movement of capital, goods and services within regional communities. Although the special regimes or zones of free movement have evolved from regional treaties establishing political and economic communities of States, they are generally relevant as manifestations of general international standards concerning permissible restrictions on internal movement and residence. There is no reason of principle to drive an artificial chasm between the imperatives of human rights on one hand, and those of the market or communities on the other hand.

(5) Internal exile or banishment is clearly governed by standards applicable to restrictions on movement and residence. However, such exile on conditions of close confinement approximate to detention or imprisonment and inevitably bring into issue the question of deprivation of liberty.

(6) In practice, issues covered by public interest grounds blend or overlap. Such grounds may thus be different expressions in different contexts of the concept of *ordre public*. The important thing is that it is international law which ultimately provides the means for scrutinizing the legality of measures taken on public interest grounds.

(7) Restrictions which were imposed by law on movement and residence within South Africa by reference to race were clearly impermissible under customary law, as elaborated by treaty standards. By these standards, discrimination in a legal sense is determined on an objective basis by reference to the justification, the reasonableness, and the proportion of the act complained of, in relation to similar rights enjoyed by groups of a different race. By the same token, any restrictions which are imposed pursuant to a policy of discrimination on any ground, including race or ethnic cleansing, are unlawful and abominable to humankind.

4

The Movement and Residence of Minorities

1. INTRODUCTION

The subject-matter of this chapter concerns the protection of minorities in the context of standards relating to freedom of movement and residence within States. The aim is to present these as additional standards for the protection of minorities in the overall context within which minorities are a specially protected category in international law.

Writing in 1950 Sir Hersh Lauterpacht[1] stated that the protection of minorities was a fundamental human right involving the preservation of peace between and within nations. The protection of minorities is also important for the maintenance of a distinct identity originating from the heritage of a people and for the development of qualities and values associated with it. This assessment remains important to the protection of minorities by the use of human rights standards concerning freedom of movement and residence law as well as to the stability of States with substantial minority populations.[2] It is argued that freedom of movement and residence is important to the protection of the identity and existence of minorities that are habitual residents of a specific area within State territory. In particular, freedom of movement may be invoked to protect minorities from being dispersed within States, or from being forcibly removed from State territory.

Apart from that, restrictions on freedom of movement of the general population may be placed delicately to give protection to the residence of minorities in areas occupied by them as a way of insulating their distinct characteristics from being eroded by others. The downside of this is that restrictions can also be applied to limit the residence and movement of minorities to 'ghettos' or in conditions less favourable to dignified habitation. So the dividing line is difficult to draw in theory and would depend on each given case which, as a minimum, would have to satisfy the requirements of non-discrimination.

Thus restrictions based on racial segregation in apartheid South Africa were unlawful and unacceptable, while in Rwanda restrictions on movement and residence would be unworkable to protect the minority Tutsis because they and the majority Hutus are integrated communities. However,

[1] Hersh Lauterpacht, *International Law and Human Rights* (London, 1950), 352.
[2] Thornberry, *International Law and the Protection of Minorities* (Oxford, 1991), ch. 5.

restrictions would be applicable to the protection of the Kosovo Albanians in the Federal Republic of Yugoslavia, the Kurds in Turkey and Iraq, the Kalahari bushmen in Botswana, the Barabaig in Tanzania, the Miskito Indians in Nicaragua, Scheduled Tribes in India, and native Indian Communities in North America.

Despite the fact that the term 'minorities' has for long been frequently used in the literature of international law, a precise and commonly agreed definition of the word 'minorities' remains elusive. When attempting an early definition in 1950, the Sub-Commission on Prevention of Discrimination and Protection of Minorities warned that for practical purposes, the term 'minorities' cannot be literally defined in simple terms.[3] According to the Sub-Commission, the term 'minority' is applicable to more or less distinct groups, living within a State, which are dominated by other groups.[4] It included elements which varied in content and form, and had acquired a restricted usage in reference to a particular kind of national or similar community which differs from the predominant group in a State. As far as the Commission was concerned, the term 'minorities' frequently applied to communities with certain ethnic, linguistic, cultural or religious characteristics and almost always to communities of a national type:

> The members of such a minority feel that they constitute a national group, or subgroup which is different from the predominant one.[5]

The Sub-Commission suggested that the term 'minority' should normally be applied to groups whose members share a common ethnic origin, language, culture or religion, and are interested in preserving either their existence as a national community or their particular distinguishing characteristics.[6]

Some attempts at a definition of the term 'minorities' combine the literal meaning with characteristics which distinguish minorities from other groups within States. The Special Rapporteur of the Sub-Commission on the Prevention of Discrimination and Protection of Minorities proposes that an ethnic, religious, or linguistic minority is a group numerically smaller than the rest of the population of the State to which it belongs and possesses cultural, physical or historical characteristics, a religion or a language different from the rest of the population.[7]

If the emphasis on the numerical element is set apart, then this definition reflects that of the Sub-Commission and the advantage is that the Sub-Commission articulates constituent elements in the definition of minorities. A useful distinction is made which touches on the degree of protection

[3] United Nations, *Definition and Classification of Minorities* (New York, 1950), 8.
[4] Ibid., 2. [5] Ibid., 9. [6] Ibid., 11.
[7] Capotorti, *Study on the Rights of Persons Belonging to Ethnic, Religious and Linguistic Minorities*, E/CN.4/Sub.2/384/Rev.1, at 7; for a critique, see Thornberry, n. 2 above, at 6–13.

required by different categories of minorities, e.g. minority groups whose members desire equality with dominant groups purely from the point of view of non-discrimination alone, and those who, in addition to claiming equality, also demand recognition of special rights.

The importance of this distinction is that special rights claimed by minorities, and the need for a stable order within the State, constitute the driving factor in the pursuit of international standards for the protection of minorities. It is perhaps in this sense that Brownlie observes that whilst the term 'minorities' is an unhappy one, the experience which has been gathered under the heading is highly relevant.[8]

In practical terms, the nature of specific claims made by minorities influences the search for suitable standards of protection. The claims include the preservation of ethnic, linguistic, religious and cultural identity on the one hand, and preservation of existence of minorities either on an individual basis, or on a group basis, on the other hand. However, the nature of the claims involved help to differentiate minorities from other groups within the population, which also make certain specific claims to protection, e.g. indigenous people.[9] The possibility of overlap in the classification of minorities and indigenous people is acknowledged:

> There is no important distinction between the goal of the minorities provisions i.e. giving extra rights to non dominant groups in a community over and above those enjoyed by the population as a whole in order to achieve a de facto equality, and granting special protection to indigenous 'backward' groups.[10]

While indigenous groups may be classified as a minority, the distinguishing factor is that claims of indigenous groups to special protection represent want of exclusive rights of protection, including land rights, in respect of specific areas inhabited by them. For instance it was objected in the Sub-Commission for the Protection and Prevention of Discrimination Against Minorities that the indigenous population of Latin America should not be recognized as a minority, but treated as a vital part of the nation and assisted in attaining the same levels of development as the rest of the community. Similar objection was made with respect to considering Australian aborigines as a minority within the meaning given to the term by the Commission.[11]

Whatever the difficulties surrounding its definition, the term 'minority' should best be regarded as one of art, laying a special recognized claim to protection, and the connotation behind it has long been established in international law. In the Advisory Opinion of 31 July 1930, the Permanent Court

[8] Brownlie, 'The Rights of Peoples in Modern International Law', in Crawford, *The Rights of Peoples* (Oxford, 1988), 16.
[9] See below Chapter 5.
[10] McKean, *Equality and Discrimination under International Law* (Oxford, 1983), 143.
[11] UN Doc. A/C 3/S.R.1103.

of International Justice set out the applicable criterion for determining what constituted a community from the point of view of minorities under the Convention of 27 November 1919 between Bulgaria and Greece.[12] The Court stated that, under the Convention, a community was a group of persons living in a given country or locality, having a race, religion, language and traditions in a sentiment of solidarity, with a view to preserving their traditions, maintaining their form of worship, securing the instruction and upbringing of their children in accordance with the spirit and traditions of their race, and mutually assisting one another. The Court pointed out that the existence of communities, and the question whether a given community conformed to this conception, were questions of fact.

In a popular statement from its Advisory Opinion in *Minority Schools in Albania*,[13] the Permanent Court of International Justice explained that the idea underlying the protection of minorities is to secure for certain elements incorporated in a State, the population of which differed from them in race, language or religion, the possibility of living peaceably alongside that population and cooperating amicably with it, while at the same time preserving the characteristics which distinguish them from the majority, and satisfying the ensuing special needs.

The term ethnic minorities embraces racial minorities. Within the United Nations, the term racial minorities fell out of favour in 1950 on grounds that it was narrow in that it referred only to inherited physical characteristics. The reason for rejection was that racial groupings were not based upon scientific facts and tended to become indistinct as a result of evolutionary processes, inter-marriage, and changes in ideas or beliefs. Thus 'ethnic' was preferred as a wider term which includes all groups possessing different biological, cultural and historical characteristics.[14] This adds confusion to the terminology and begs the question of what constitutes 'ethnic'? It may very well be that the classification 'racial minorities' was rejected on grounds of political correctness.

With this background in mind, the chapter begins by examining standards of general application to the protection of minorities. It then proceeds to consider the application of Article 27 of the Covenant on Civil and Political Rights in the context of restrictions on freedom of internal movement and residence. It ends by examining standards concerning special measures for the protection of collective interests of minorities and the

[12] P.C.I.J., Series B, No. 17, at 19, 21, 22 and 23. The Convention in question related to the emigration of certain minority communities between Bulgaria and Greece. It put into effect Article 56(2) of the Peace Treaty of 27 November 1919 between the Allied and Associated Powers and Bulgaria. This article formed part of the provisions relating to the protection of minorities.

[13] (1935) P.C.I.J. Ser.A/B, No. 64, at 17.

[14] McKean, *Equality and Discrimination*, n. 10 above, at 144, Capotorti, *Study*, n. 7 above, at 144.

relevance of restrictions on the movement and residence of persons within States.

2. GENERAL STANDARDS OF PROTECTION OF MINORITIES

Concern about the protection of minorities in certain European States following the First World War marked the earliest international system of protecting human rights under the League of Nations. The League established a sensitive regime designed to protect minorities against discrimination and to ensure their enjoyment of civil rights in newly reconstituted and enlarged States as part of the process of restoring international peace at the Peace Conference of 1919.

Standards for the protection of minorities were formulated in a series of treaties called the Minorities Treaties. These treaties were entered into between the Allied and Associated Powers, and certain States which were created or reconstituted after the First World War.[15] The Minorities Treaties were concluded alongside the peace treaties and guaranteed by the League of Nations following the First World War. They made provision for the protection of the civil and political rights of members of ethnic, religious and linguistic minorities.[16] The Treaties were mostly similar in content, particularly as regards the protection of rights to life, liberty, equality before the law and in the exercise of civil and political rights.[17] Principles enunciated in the Treaties underpinned the equality of treatment of minorities in the sense of non-discrimination, and recognition of special rights of persons who belonged to minority groups. It is these principles which retain a particular significance to the protection of the rights of minorities in international law.

(i) Non-discrimination and the protection of minorities

With respect to the application of principles for the protection of minorities under the Treaties, Judge Tanaka underscored the point that what is protected is not the religious or linguistic group as a whole, but the

[15] The Allied and Associated Powers were: the USA, the then British Empire, France, Italy and Japan. The States included Poland, the Greek, Romanian, and Serbian Kingdoms.

[16] The five main treaties were: Treaty Between Principal Allied and Associated Powers and Poland signed at Versailles on 28 June 1919; Treaty Between the Principal Allied and Associated Powers and Czechoslovakia signed at Saint-Germane-en-Laye on 10 September 1919; Treaty Between the Principal Allied and Associated Powers and Serb-Croat-Slovene State signed at Saint-Germaine-en-Laye on 10 September 1919; Treaty Between the Principal Allied and Associated Powers and Romania signed at Paris on 9 December 1919; Treaty Concerning the Protection of Minorities in Greece signed at Sevres on 10 August 1920.

[17] Brownlie, *Principles of Public International Law*, 5th edn. (Oxford, 1998), 569–70; Jennings and Watts, *Oppenheim's International Law*, 9th edn. (London, 1996), 972–7.

individuals belonging to the group.[18] This point had been emphasized earlier by the Permanent Court of International Justice in its interpretation of the Greco-Bulgarian Convention.[19] The Court emphasized that the Convention indicated clearly that it was individuals who were entitled to take advantage of its terms, and that the Convention applied only to persons who formed a minority, and not to minorities generally. McKean[20] maintains that the principle of non-discrimination under the Treaties was negative in that it did not require individuals to take positive action collectively to establish their rights. He echoes the general view that it merely guaranteed to persons belonging to racial, linguistic or religious minorities the right not to be discriminated against in the exercise of civil and political rights as enjoyed equally by other persons.

However, certain special guarantees could be exercised by members of minorities acting together in the hope that they would be pacified and content with their new environment.[21] For instance, the Treaties conferred special rights in matters of monetary benefits from public funds. In towns or districts where minorities were considerably present, provision was made in the Treaties to assure them of an equitable share in the enjoyment and application of monies provided out of public funds for educational, religious or charitable purposes.[22] Several important interpretations regarding the application of the principle of non-discrimination in relation to special rights of protection of minorities were made by the Permanent Court of International Justice. In its Advisory Opinion in the case of *Minority Schools in Albania*, the Court alluded to two factors which it regarded as particularly necessary to attain the objective of protecting minorities. These were:

(a) to ensure that nationals belonging to racial, religious or linguistic minorities were placed in every respect on a footing of perfect equality with the other nationals of the State; and
(b) to ensure for the minority elements suitable means for the preservation of their racial peculiarities, traditions and national characteristics.

According to the Court, these two requirements were closely linked in the sense that there would be no true equality between a majority and a minority if the latter were deprived of its own institutions, and consequently compelled to renounce that which constitutes the very essence of its being a minority.

Under the principle of non-discrimination, a difference of treatment is permissible in order to attain positive equality between groups. Judge

[18] *South West African* cases *(2nd Phase)*, 308.
[19] P.C.I.J., Series B, No. 17 at 3.
[20] McKean, *Equality and Discrimination*, n. 10 above, at 24.
[21] Ibid.
[22] Capotorti, *Study*, n. 7 above, at 19.

Tanaka[23] made reference to permissible and impermissible discrimination in the context of the Mandates which were established under the League of Nations. The Mandate system was a form of minority regime and the Trusteeship system under the Charter of the United Nations is a strong analogy. Judge Tanaka noted forthrightly that the spirit of the Minorities Treaty was positive and permissive on the basis that the norm of non-discrimination was a reverse side of the notion of equality. It prohibited a State from excluding members of a minority group from participating in rights, interests and opportunities which a majority of the population enjoy.

The Judge inferred that a difference of treatment with respect to minorities is reasonably required by the differences of religion, education, and even custom:

> The rights guaranteed to members of a minority group is for the purpose of the protection of their interests in order to cultivate their own religious, educational or linguistic values as a recognition of their fundamental rights rather than the motive of discrimination itself.[24]

It is clear that no specific provision concerning the right of movement and residence in areas inhabited by minorities was included in the Treaties. But the Permanent Court of International Justice took a broad view of the concept of civil rights under the Minorities Treaties. The concept included rights acquired under a contract for the possession or use of moveable and immoveable property,[25] and some legal arrangements for the protection of minorities seem to have taken into account their freedom of movement to gain access to certain strategic areas. Such arrangements were evident in the creation of the Free City of Danzig and in the protection of Polish minorities who resided in that City.

The Permanent Court of International Justice explained that since the separation of Danzig from Germany was contrary to the wishes of the German people, and virtually the whole population of that City was German, the Peace Conference decided to make Danzig a Free City without incorporating it in Poland in order to assure access to the sea.[26] Such access included freedom of movement on the part of German inhabitants of the city. Moreover, the concept of liberty under the Minorities Treaties may, in its ordinary meaning, be taken to encapsulate the freedom of movement of individuals within the context set by the minorities regime.

As already stated, freedom of movement is a species of liberty.[27] And the

[23] *South West African* cases (2nd Phase) at 307–10.

[24] Ibid., at 307.

[25] *Advisory Opinion on Certain Questions Relating to Settlers of German Origin in the Territory Ceded by Germany to Poland* (1923) P.C.I.J. at 23.

[26] *Treatment of Polish Nationals and other Persons of Polish Origin or Speech in the Danzig Territory* (1932) P.C.I.J., Ser. A/B No.44, at 27–8.

[27] See above Chapter 2.

authoritative categorization of rights now acknowledged as belonging to the species of civil and political rights under the Covenant on Civil and Political Rights includes freedom of movement and residence within States. Under the Treaties, the status given to the principles protecting minorities was that they were fundamental and, no law, regulation, or official action was to conflict or interfere with or prevail over them.[28] According to the Treaties, these principles constituted obligations of international concern placed under the guarantee of the League of Nations.[29] Any dispute arising from the obligations regarding the protection of persons belonging to racial, religious, or linguistic minorities was to be held as a dispute of an international character.[30]

In the present state of international law, the language in which these obligations were expressed, i.e. 'obligations of international concern' giving rise to 'a dispute of an international character', would be sufficient to categorize them as *erga omnes*, except that the limited normative character of the Treaties in question rendered them incapable of attaining such a status in any case.

To place the Treaties in perspective, they were exceptional as special arrangements for the protection of minorities imposed upon vanquished States. They were placed under the guarantee of the League of Nations as a condition for territorial settlements in the aftermath of the First World War. Whereas the Treaties had normative value between the parties, they were not capable of generating general standards of application outside of their treaty context. Whether or not the demise of the League of Nations rendered the principles for the protection of persons belonging to minorities extinct should now be considered as a moot question. In a study conducted in 1950,[31] the United Nations argued that the system of protection of minorities under the Minorities Treaties had ceased to exist. Arguments presented by the Secretariat of the United Nations in this study may be summarized in three parts:

(a) first, that the whole minorities regime in 1919 was an integral part of the system established to regulate the outcome of the First World War and create the League of Nations. One principle of that system was that certain States only, i.e. newly reconstituted or enlarged, should be subject to obligations and international control in the matter of minorities;

(b) secondly, that from the strictly legal point of view, the formal liquidation of the war had been completed by the conclusion of peace treaties. The provisions of such treaties, and the opinions expressed

[28] Article 1 of the Treaty of Versailles.

[29] Ibid., Article 12. [30] Ibid., Article 14.

[31] *Study of the Legal Validity of the Undertakings Concerning Minorities*, E/CN.4/367, ch. XIV.

by their authors imply that the former minorities protection regime had ceased to exist so far as concerned former enemy states with which those treaties had been concluded;

(c) thirdly, the whole system of minorities protection was overthrown by the Second World War. After this, and since 1945, a different philosophy ushered in the idea of a general protection of human rights and fundamental freedoms.

The position taken by writers is that the Minorities Treaties were superseded by the principle of universal respect for human rights and fundamental freedoms for all which the Charter of the United Nations introduced in 1945.[32] A more persuasive view is that the conduct of the States parties to the Treaties since the Second World War evidenced a general desire for the Treaties to be terminated. It is plausible to conclude that the parties considered the obligations under the Treaties as not having any continuing binding force:

> The fact that no state disputed the findings of the study nor made any real attempt to have the issue debated, though it appeared for several years on the Commission's agenda is evidence of a general, tacit agreement that the minorities treaties were no longer in force.[33]

However, a fair assessment of the value of the Minorities Treaties must acknowledge that they exerted tremendous influence towards the establishment of an international system for the protection of human rights. The treaties were, retrospectively speaking, hostages of fortune. Their proper place in international legal history is that they were precursors to the present international system of protection of human rights which has developed under the Charter of the United Nations. Upon its adoption in 1945, the Charter of the United Nations stated, as one of its purposes, the promotion and encouragement of respect for human rights and fundamental freedoms without distinction as to race, sex, language, or religion. It made no special rules for the protection of the rights of minorities as such.

The assumption was that once the principle of universal respect for human rights was accepted, it became unnecessary to include specific rules for the protection of minorities within the Charter. After all, the reasons for objecting to the inclusion of a regime for the protection of minorities in the Charter were the same as those presented against enumeration of specific human rights and the establishment of a system of international protection of human rights within the Charter.

The lack of provisions for the protection of minorities in the Universal Declaration of Human Rights, and in the Charter of the United Nations,

[32] McKean, *Equality and Discrimination*, n. 10 above, at 46, n. 2; Thornberry, n. 2 above, at 113–23.

[33] McKean, ibid., 46–7.

did not mean that the protection of minorities was no longer fundamental in international law. The assumption was that the universal system of protecting human rights would afford protection to minorities as well. This approach was apparently faulty, given that the existence of minorities and States is often inter-twined. When the Universal Declaration of Human Rights was adopted, there was unease expressed at the universal formula of protection. While the General Assembly resolutely stated that it could not remain indifferent to the fate of minorities,[34] it pointed out the difficulties of adopting a uniform solution of 'this complex and delicate question, which has special aspects in each State in which it arose'. The omission of principles dealing with minorities in the Universal Declaration of Human Rights owed more to the lack of consensus on how best to deal with the diversity of the problem, and must not be confused with rejection of the concept of protection of minorities.[35]

One of the main assumptions in the Charter was that prescription of the standard of equality of treatment would in effect embrace the protection of rights of members of minority groups. Throughout the Charter, there is much emphasis placed on the principle of non-discrimination and the affirmation of equality for all.[36] It is least arguable that the prohibition of non-discrimination on grounds of race, colour, sex, language, religion, political or other opinion, national or social origin, property, birth or other status is a norm of general international law.[37] So, whether or not there are any special rules dealing with ethnic minorities within the Charter, the fact remains that minorities are beneficiaries of the general standards pertaining to non-discrimination,[38] but the main question to be asked is whether these standards are sufficiently adequate to give effective protection to minorities, and whether diluting the specific attention paid to minorities in favour of general human rights prescriptions not only lost the strength of protection afforded to minorities, but also failed to handle, with tragic consequences, the more specific challenges to the protection of minorities presented by the dissolution of the Federal Republic of Yugoslavia, the former Soviet Union, and Czechoslovakia.

The categories of race, origin, and nationality were specifically included in the Charter as grounds upon which discrimination is prohibited in order to establish the universal principle of protection, including that of minorities. Capotorti's argument that since 1945, the principle of non-

[34] Gen. Ass. Res. 217 C (III) of 10 December 1948 on the Fate of Minorities.

[35] On its part, the United Nations explicitly signalled its commitment to taking effective measures for the protection of racial, national, religious or linguistic minorities. For this purpose, it referred to the Economic and Social Council of the United Nations to ask the Commission on Human Rights and the Sub-Commission on the Prevention of Discrimination and Protection of Minorities to make a thorough study of the problem.

[36] Articles 13(b), 55(4), 62(2), 76(c).

[37] See above Chapter 2.

[38] See, e.g., Article 14 of the European Convention on Human Rights.

discrimination has been included in the context of the protection of human rights and fundamental freedoms of all human beings, and not in the context of measures designed to protect minorities, amounts to a fragmentation of general human rights standards. Ironic as this may seem, his well-acclaimed study endorses the relevancy of the principles concerning the protection of minorities in the context of contemporary human rights standards. A pertinent question to consider in this regard is whether there are special standards justifying positive measures of protection of minorities in order to maintain and preserve characteristics of their group identity. This begs discussion of the content of Article 27 of the Covenant on Civil and Political Rights.

3. PROTECTION OF MINORITIES UNDER ARTICLE 27 OF THE COVENANT

Article 27 of the Covenant constitutes evidence of general principles of international law concerning the protection of minorities. It provides that:

> In those states in which ethnic, religious or linguistic minorities exist, persons belonging to such minorities shall not be denied the right, in community with the other members of their group, to enjoy their own culture, to profess and practice their own religion, or to use their language.

The preparatory work of the Covenant reveals the intention behind the design of this provision.[39] The words 'in those states in which ethnic, religious or linguistic minorities exist' were used in reference to persons belonging to minority groups which were well defined, separate or distinct and long established on the territory of a State. They were intended to exclude foreign nationals resident in State territory from the scope of application of Article 27. The phrase 'persons belonging to such minorities shall not be denied the right' was intended to limit the obligations of States to permitting minorities to exercise rights to enjoy, profess, and practise their own culture, religion, and use of language in community with others.

Inclusion of the words 'in community with others' qualifies the enjoyment of rights by individual persons in such a way that they are subject to the rights of other members of a minority group. This qualification probably seeks to maintain a balance between individual members of a minority group in the exercise of their rights. The scope of Article 27 is concerned with rights of persons belonging to ethnic, religious, and linguistic

[39] See Bossuyt, *Guide to The Travaux Preparatoires to the International Covenant on Civil and Political Rights* (Dordrecht, 1987), 494–6; Sohn, 'The Rights of Minorities' in Henkin, *The International Bill of Rights. The Covenant on Civil and Political Rights* (New York, 1981), 273–4; Capotorti, *Study*, n. 7 above, 32–4.

minorities. According to the Inter-American Commission on Human Rights, Article 27 obliges State parties to allow persons who belong to these groups to enjoy their own culture, to profess and practise their own religion and to use their own language.[40]

International lawyers have been concerned to illuminate the nature of the protection afforded to minorities under Article 27.[41] Brownlie has observed that Article 27 provides a static guarantee.[42] McKean remarks that the wording 'persons . . . shall not be denied the right . . . to enjoy their own culture' does not *prima facie* place any positive obligation on States to adopt legislative measures or undertake expenditure. McKean further relates Article 27 to certain rights in the Covenant on Economic Social and Cultural Rights[43] which impose positive obligations on States in educational and cultural spheres and argues that the proper context of Article 27 requires States to adopt legislative and administrative measures to enable its objectives to be achieved. In his view, conservation of a group's culture and language can only be guaranteed by establishing certain institutions for its benefit:

> If Art. 27 does not require positive measures it is not easy to see how it adds anything to the general equality and non discrimination provision of Art. 2(1) [of the Covenant on Civil and Political Rights]. Art. 27 must be interpreted as an additional provision to ensure for members of minorities, in the context of the other rights set out in the Covenant, the right to special protection to practise their own culture, language and religion.[44]

James Crawford's[45] view that Article 27 hovers between individual and group rights is a balanced description of that provision. As well as guaranteeing individual members of minority groups the right to profess their own religion, culture, and language, the words 'in community with others' may have the effect of permitting positive action to preserve the cultural, religious and linguistic values of minorities.

This view is supported by the pronouncements of the Inter-American Commission in relation to the protection of ethnic groups of the Atlantic Zone of Nicaragua. The Commission has expressed the view that Article 27 reaffirms the need to protect ethnic groups and establishes additional protection for them beyond that granted to the other nationals of a State in order to bring true equality among them. In this connection, the Commission appraises the necessity for special legal protection of ethnic

[40] IACHR, *Report on the Situation of Human Rights of a Segment of the Nicaraguan Population of Miskito Origin* (DEA/Ser./V/II. 62, doc. 26, 1984), 30. See also Capotorti, *Study*, n. 7 above, 35; Sohn, 'The Rights of Minorities', n. 39 above, 275.

[41] Thornberry, n. 2 above, ch. 23.

[42] Brownlie, 'The Rights of Peoples', n. 8 above, 3.

[43] Articles 13–15.

[44] McKean, *Equality and Discrimination*, n. 10 above, 145, for a contrary view.

[45] Crawford, *The Rights of Peoples*, n. 8 above, 60.

groups in matters of language, observation of their religion, and all aspects that are generally related to the preservation of their cultural values or identity.[46]

The Commission went further to acknowledge that, in addition to such special protection, it was fundamental for members of an ethnic group to be allowed to enjoy all the rights set forth by the American Convention in order to guarantee their functioning as a group. Certain rights were determined by the Commission to be relevant to the protection of the honour and dignity of minorities, i.e., freedom of thought and expression, the right of assembly and association, the right to movement and residence, and the right of minorities to elect their authorities. The Commission pertinently observed that aspects associated with the productive organization of minorities, including the issue of the ancestral and communal lands, should be added to these rights. However, it is usually the case that claims of ethnic minorities do not extend to traditional territories, as do those of indigenous groups.[47]

The range of legal opinion surveyed regarding the content of Article 27 supports the proposition that the principles contained in that provision are essential to the preservation of group identity, and the maintenance of real equality of status with the rest of the population in matters of culture, language and religion. Arguably, Article 27, read in the context of the Covenant as a whole, incorporates the principle of justified and proportionate differential treatment in relation to members of ethnic, religious and linguistic minorities on grounds of identity and equality.

Recent developments in the protection of minorities place more *active* obligations upon States in the protection of minorities. Article 4 of the Framework Convention for the Protection of Minorities in Europe 1995[48] obliges States, where necessary, to undertake adequate measures in order to promote full and effective equality between persons belonging to minorities and those belonging to the majority in all areas of economic, social and cultural life. Under Article 1 of the Declaration of Persons Belonging to National or Ethnic, Religious and Linguistic Minorities 1992:[49] 'States shall protect the existence and the national or ethnic, cultural, religious identity of minorities within their respective territories and shall encourage conditions for the promotion of that identity'.

There is less equivocation in the Framework Convention on the issue of the protection of minorities as a category, and of individual rights of persons belonging to minorities. Thus Article 1 recognizes the protection of national minorities and of the rights and freedoms of persons belonging to those minorities. In terms of Article 3, persons belonging to minorities may exercise the rights and enjoy the freedom flowing from the principles enshrined

[46] IACHR, *Report on the Situation*, n. 40 above, 29. [47] See below Chapter 5.
[48] (1995) 34 I.L.M. 351. [49] (1993) 32 I.L.M. 911.

in the Convention individually as well as in community with others. The Declaration contains the same principle, except that its general tenor is inclined towards minorities as individuals much more than the Convention. Both standards are related however; the Convention is a follow up to the Vienna Declaration on Human Rights 1993[50] which, in turn, draws inspiration—in relation to minorities—from the Declaration on Minorities. The development of positive obligations for the protection of minorities is to be welcomed as an advancement on the scope of human rights and a contribution towards the stability of States.

4. PROTECTION OF MINORITIES AND RESTRICTION OF MOVEMENT AND RESIDENCE

International standards concerning restrictions which are permissible to limit the movement and residence of persons within States are obviously applicable to the protection of minorities. Observations made above by the Inter-American Commission in reference to the rights which are relevant to the protection of the honour and dignity of ethnic minorities include the right of movement and residence within States.

Broadly speaking, restrictions are essential to the protection of special measures and the collective existence of minorities who habitually reside in a specific area of State territory. They are also useful in providing safeguards against the forced assimilation of such minorities.

The precise mode of application of standards concerning such restrictions in the context of the protection of minorities under Article 27 and the principle of non-discrimination is evident in the decision of the Human Rights Committee in *Sandra Lovelace v Canada*. Restrictions which were in issue in this case were placed as a special measure of protection of Malisset Indians who resided on the Tobique Reserve. In its decision, the Committee expressed the view that restrictions on movement and residence are permissible for the purpose of protection of interests of minorities from the point of view of Article 27 of the Covenant.

The Committee considered that restriction of the movement and residence of non-Indians on the Reserve was justifiable under Article 12(3) of the Covenant. It further stated that restriction of the movement and residence of the Indians to the Reserve was also justified. In its view, restrictions upon residence on reserves to certain categories of persons entitled to live on a reserve are necessitated by purposes such as protection of its resources and preservation of its people.[51]

The supposition that the special rules for the protection of minorities

[50] U.N. Doc., A/CONF.157/23, 12 July 1993.

[51] *Sandra Lovelace v Canada*, Communication No. 22/77, *Selected Decisions under The Optional Protocol* (Second to Sixteenth Sessions) (New York, 1985), at 87.

under Article 27, if they be accepted as such, are connected with other human rights standards contained in the Covenant is supported by the views of the Committee. It determined that statutory restrictions affecting the right to residence on a reserve of a person belonging to the minority concerned must have both a reasonable and objective justification in the sense of positive discrimination and be consistent with the other provisions of the Covenant read as a whole.

This means that Article 27 must be construed and applied in the light of the other provisions such as Article 12 (on freedom of movement and residence), Article 17 (interference with privacy, family, home or correspondence) and Article 23 (protection of the family) in so far as these may be relevant to the particular case. Provisions against discrimination, such as Articles 2, 3, and 26, were singled out by the Committee as applicable to Article 27.[52]

The views of the Committee in *Sandra Lovelace v Canada* provide authority for the proposition that the principle of the protection of minorities under Article 27 of the Covenant on Civil and Political Rights is related to the principle of non-discrimination. The effect of this is that for the purpose of protection of the rights in Article 27, differential treatment is permissible to minorities in order to grant them substantial equality of status with the other population groups.

5. RESTRICTIONS ON MOVEMENT AND RESIDENCE AND PROTECTION OF MINORITY GROUPS

International standards pertaining to restrictions upon the movement and residence of persons within States appear to be relevant to the protection of the collective rights of minorities. This claim is founded on two grounds. The first ground is that restrictions are permitted for the protection of the rights and freedoms of others under Article 12(3) of the Covenant on Civil and Political Rights. It is considered that the words 'rights and freedoms of others' is broad enough to cover protection of rights of diverse categories of persons or groups generally. In the context of the protection of rights of minorities, the phrase 'rights and freedoms of others' may be interpreted literally to mean rights of individual members belonging to minority groups, or the rights of minority groups as such.

Restrictions can thus be permitted as part of the protection of minority groups in certain areas inhabited by these groups in order to prohibit certain categories of people from moving into and residing in those areas. That this standard is of general application is supported by its inclusion in Article 2 of the Fourth Protocol to the European Convention on Human Rights; and Article 2 expressly permits restrictions upon movement and

[52] Ibid.

residence in particular areas. Such restrictions are highly relevant to the protection of those minority groups which seek a certain amount of autonomy within the State, such as the Indians of the Atlantic Zone in Nicaragua.

The second ground is based on special measures for the protection and advancement of racial and ethnic minorities under the Convention on the Elimination of All Forms of Racial Discrimination. Article 1(4) of the Convention introduces the principle of special measures as a qualification to the definition of non-discrimination. It states that:

> Special measures taken for the sole purpose of securing adequate advancement of certain racial or ethnic groups or individuals requiring such protection as may be necessary in order to ensure such groups or individuals equal enjoyment of or exercise of human rights and fundamental freedoms shall not be deemed racial discrimination, provided, however, that such measures do not, as a consequence, lead to the maintenance of separate rights for different racial groups and that they shall not be continued after the objectives for which they were taken have been achieved.

The qualification made by this provision excludes from the definition of racial discrimination those distinctions, exclusions, restrictions or preferences which are made for the sole purpose of securing the advancement of certain racial or ethnic groups or individuals. As the High Court of Australia has observed, Article 1(4) of the Convention proceeds on the premise that certain groups or individuals may require protection in order to ensure to them equal enjoyment or exercise of human rights and fundamental freedoms. The High Court also noted that, but for some such provision, the giving of this form of protection would, in some situations at least, amount to racial discrimination.[53]

Special measures are therefore objectively justified from the perspective of international human rights standards concerning discrimination. Article 2(2) of the Convention on the Elimination of All Forms of Racial Discrimination translates the principle of special measures into an international obligation:

> States Parties shall, when the circumstances so warrant, take in the social, economic, cultural and other fields, special or concrete measures to ensure the adequate development and protection of certain racial groups or individuals belonging to them, for the purpose of guaranteeing them the full and equal enjoyment of human rights and fundamental freedoms. These measures shall in no case entail as a consequence the maintenance of unequal or separate rights for different racial groups after the objectives for which they were taken have been achieved.

In *Gerhardy v Brown*, Mr Justice Brenan[54] shed some light on the meaning of a special measure. He conceded that a special measure is *ex hypothesi*, discriminatory in character; it denies formal equality in

[53] *Gerhardy v Brown* (1985) 57 A.L.R. 472, at 497.

[54] Ibid., at 517, 520.

order to achieve effective and genuine equality. In this view, a special measure:

(a) confers a benefit on some or all members of a class;
(b) the membership of which is based on race, colour, descent, or national or ethnic origin;
(c) for the sole purpose of securing adequate advancement of the beneficiaries in order that they may enjoy and exercise equally with others human rights and fundamental freedoms;
(d) in circumstances where the protection given to the beneficiaries by the special measure is necessary in order that they may enjoy and exercise equally with others human rights and fundamental freedoms.

Reflecting the position taken by the Inter-American Commission on Human Rights, Justice Brenan cautions that special measures for the advancement of a racial group must not be imposed arbitrarily; the wishes of the beneficiaries of the measure are of great importance, if not essential to determining whether a measure is taken for the purpose of securing their advancement.[55]

So far as the protection of minorities is concerned, restrictions in the form of special measures are permissible to preserve certain collective characteristics of minorities. Justice Brenan[56] explains that:

> A racial minority which wishes to preserve its own identity may need particular supports to preserve that identity if its members are not to be disadvantaged in the society of which it is a part. If such a racial minority is denied those supports, its members may not only lose their own sense of identity but be unable to adopt the standards and customs of the majority or cope with the pressures which assimilation with the majority entails.

By definition, special measures of protection of group or individual rights are meant to be temporary and there is authoritative consensus for this view. Justice Murphy has observed that the proviso in Article 1(4) of the Convention on the Elimination of All Forms of Racial Discrimination looked primarily to measures of a temporary character which would alleviate the disadvantages under which the people of a particular race laboured at a particular stage in their evolution.[57]

Justice Brenan echoes a similar view and states that such special arrangements are compensatory to disadvantaged groups or individuals.[58] McKean thinks that special measures envisage crash programmes which allow special privileges or preferences to underdeveloped groups and must cease when members of the group in question achieve a real *de facto* equality with the rest of the community.[59] The real problem lies in determining the

[55] Ibid., at 521. [56] Ibid., at 522. [57] Ibid., at 498. [58] Ibid., at 517.
[59] McKean, *Equality and Discrimination*, n. 10 above, 159.

stage at which such equality has been attained and when the special measures must be discontinued. If the measures in question are effected as an executive act, then they may be revoked as a matter of political judgement. However, special measures involving restriction of movement and residence are required under international standards to be effected by means of statutory law. In such cases, the statute may have to contain conditions stipulating for the revocation of the measures in question once the conditions are met.

In *Gerhardy v Brown*, the High Court of Australia faced the difficulty of attempting to reconcile a legislative regime of special measures with international standards requiring their discontinuance after achieving the objectives for which they were taken. The legislation in question was the Land Act which vested title to certain lands, and exclusive right of movement and residence on such lands, to a group of persons known as the Pitjantjatjara. The Act did not stipulate conditions by which the measures contained in it could be regarded as having been fulfilled, or when they could be discontinued.

The Court noted that the legislation in question had about it an air of permanence. In the opinion of the Court, the fact that the legislation was styled to continue to enforce the special measures indefinitely did not involve an infringement of the proviso requiring that the measures be discontinued after meeting the objectives for which they were brought into force:

> What it requires is a discontinuance of the special measures after the achievement of the objectives for which they were taken. It does not insist on discontinuance if discontinuance will bring about a failure of the objectives which justify the taking of special measures in the first place.[60]

The Court explained the indefinite character of the Land Act by reference to the fact that it would be a problem for the legislation to specify a terminal point in the operation of the regime which it introduced. It suggested that the validity of the special measures under the Act would only come into question if it were shown that the special measures had ceased to be consistent with the requirements of Article 1(4) of the Convention.

In other words, factual or objective evidence regarding the circumstances of the beneficiary group is required to demonstrate that such a group is no longer disadvantaged in comparison with the rest of the population. In the opinion of the Court, such a question could only be answered in the fullness of time and in the light of future development:[61]

> What the provisions (of the Convention) are concerned to avoid, however, is the maintenance of separate rights after the objectives have been achieved and the con-

[60] *Gerhardy v Brown*, n. 53 above, at 498; see also Justice Brenan at 525.
[61] Per Judge Murphy at 498; Judge Wilson at 504; and Judge Brenan at 518.

tinuation of special measures after that time. The provisions are satisfied if, when that time arrives, separate rights are repealed and special measures are discontinued. As it is impossible to determine in time when the objectives of a special measure will be achieved, the better construction of the provisos is that they contemplate that a State Party will keep its special measures under review, and that the measure will lose the character of a special measure at the time when its objectives have been achieved. But the provisions do not require the time for the operation of a special measure to be defined before the objectives of the special measure have been achieved. With the passage of time, circumstances may no longer warrant the continuation of some or all of those provisions of the Land Rights Act which provide for formal discrimination.[62]

Some States, for example, Tunisia, and Algeria, disapprove of such special measures on grounds that they establish a privileged status for some groups and amount to some form of rigid separation between different groups. In political terms, special measures look like apartheid, and governments are sensitive to the potential threat to the cohesion of States. However, as the Permanent Court put it, the intent of the principles for the protection of minorities is to eliminate a dangerous source of oppression, recrimination and dispute, and to prevent racial and religious hatreds from having free play to the detriment of the State.

Many of the so-called conflicts of tribalism in Africa are in truth demands for special protection against domination by other groups and signal the failure to promote a stable policy of co-existence between heterogeneous groups. The creation of special regimes for the protection of certain minority groups, not simply Tribal Trust Lands inherited from colonialism, is particularly desirable to preserve stability within African States.

In the case of ethnic groups of the Atlantic Zone of Nicaragua, the Inter-American Commission recommended that Nicaragua should give recognition to some form of autonomy and limited self-determination on the part of Miskitos within Nicaragua:

it is fundamental to establishing new conditions for co-existence between the ethnic minorities and the Government of Nicaragua, in order to settle historic antagonisms . . . in the opinion of the IACHR, the need to preserve and guarantee the observance of these principles in practice entails the need to establish an adequate institutional order as part of the structure of the Nicaraguan state. Such an institutional organisation can only effectively carry out its assigned purposes to the extent that it is designed in the context of broad consultation, and carried out with the direct participation of the ethnic minorities of Nicaragua, through their freely chosen representatives.[63]

The Commission thus rejected forced assimilation of ethnic groups into the rest of the population and cautioned that the results could be disastrous.

[62] Judge Brenan at 525.

[63] IACHR, *Report on the Situation*, n. 40 above, 33.

Restrictions affecting special measures of protection which limit the movement and residence of persons or groups not belonging to ethnic minorities in areas occupied by the latter should also be seen in the light of the standards contained in the Convention on the Prevention and Punishment of the Crime of Genocide 1948. This Convention prohibits acts committed with intent to destroy, in whole or in part, a national, ethnic, racial or religious group and protects these groups from physical destruction on grounds of their nationality, ethnicity, race or religion. Standards in the Genocide Convention fall in the purview of general international standards and the protection accorded to minority groups under its terms is enhanced by the establishment of international tribunals (former Yugoslavia and Rwanda) in 1993 and 1994 respectively with jurisdiction to punish crimes against humanity, as well as genocide.

6. CONCLUSIONS

(1) While the principle of non-discrimination remains an effective legal basis for the protection of minorities in matters of culture, language, religion, and other characteristics essential to the preservation of the lifestyle of minority groups, it is inadequate to deal with claims where the autonomy of minorities is the appropriate form of protection.

(2) In this context, the standards relating to freedom of movement and residence together with the attendant regime of restrictions are applicable to fortify the protection of rights of minorities under Article 27 of the Covenant on Civil and Political Rights.

(3) Since Article 27 provides for additional rights to those set out in the Covenant, it must be seen as representing an attempt at establishing a limited special regime for minorities protection under current human rights standards, but its inadequacy is shown in the effort to articulate additional standards aimed at providing additional measures of protection at the European and United Nations levels.

(4) These standards would appear to place positive international obligations to protect minorities, thus transforming the negative or static character of Article 27.

(5) Standards concerning restrictions on the movement and residence of persons are applicable under Article 27 in the context of special measures which require limitation of movement and residence as a means of preserving the existence and identity of minorities.

(6) Such standards may be effected on the ground which permits restrictions for the protection of rights of others, provided that the rights in question are understood as referring to the rights of minorities.

(7) However, quite apart from the context of Article 27, restrictions on

movement and residence within States are permissible as part of special measures for the advancement of certain disadvantaged racial and ethnic groups under the Convention for the Elimination of All Forms of Racial Discrimination.

(8) Restrictions made in the context of this Convention are applicable to the protection of both group and individual rights. Although Article 27 hovers between these categories, it clearly does not recognize minority groups as an entity. The emergent standards would do well to move towards the recognition of certain minorities as groups or communities.

(9) Where special measures for the advancement of racial or ethnic groups involve restrictions on movement and residence, the legislation enabling such measures must contain conditions stipulating for the revocation of the measures in question when circumstances warrant such action.

(10) Nevertheless, there remains the difficulty of the compliance of such a piece of legislation with international standards requiring that special measures be discontinued after fulfilling their objectives.

(11) Special measures which have an 'air of permanence' are contrary to the very essence of special measures. By definition, these are temporary and compensatory measures which are given in order to assist disadvantaged ethnic or racial groups to redress their state of imbalance in the enjoyment of human rights and fundamental freedoms. The criterion of temporariness is important if special measures are not to be seen to be discriminatory. But there could be inherent political problems arising from the continuity or discontinuity of special measures.

(12) However, special measures which are effected in accordance with international standards concerning the protection of disadvantaged ethnic groups have a reasonable objective and are thus justifiable.

5

Exclusive Movement and Residence of Indigenous People on Traditional Lands

1. INTRODUCTION

Restrictions on the entry and residence of non-indigenous persons on State territory traditionally occupied by indigenous groups are sometimes used to protect certain collective rights of indigenous groups, such as identity or distinct lifestyle which by definition are connected with traditional lands. The difficulty, however, is that claims to collective rights, let alone the rights of indigenous groups, have not always been appreciated as part of international standards of human rights.

This is due to the fact that human rights in contemporary international law generally tend to be conceived in terms of individual rights. The reason for this is that the drive towards formulating international standards for the protection of human rights unavoidably carried with it the leading Western nations' ideology of the freedom of the individual as the centre of protection. As a result, the classical formulations of human rights contained in standard-setting instruments of general application omitted reference to rights of groups as such, with the exception, perhaps, of self-determination.

The collection of distinguished essays in the *Rights of Peoples* reveals the shortcomings of international law in relation to the protection of rights of groups:

> The present international legal framework does not give access to the main political arenas to the representatives of indigenous groups themselves, nor does it seem to deal with their specific historic identity, their special claims, nor with their special value to human society as a whole.[1]

However, there is support for the proposition that, in general, the concept of human rights also includes group rights. Judge Mason[2] has stated that the concept of human rights, though generally associated in Western thought with the rights of individuals, also extends to the rights of peoples and the preservation of their cultures. In support of this view, Judge Mason notes that municipal legislative action having the purpose and effect of reserving

[1] Falk, 'The Rights of Peoples (In Particular Indigenous Peoples)' in Crawford, *The Rights of Peoples* (Oxford, 1988), 31.

[2] Per Justice Mason in *Gerhardy v Brown* (1985) 57 A.L.R. 472, at 497.

land for indigenous peoples and prohibiting its acquisition by others is not uncommon. Brownlie lends weight to the idea that groups of people as such have certain collective rights inherent in the concepts of equality and of human rights.[3]

Indeed, the Charter of the United Nations which forms the basis of human rights norms in general international law speaks of the equality of States and peoples. This at once provides the source for the existence of rights of peoples either on the basis, or in the context, of equality. And beginning in 1957, with the adoption of the International Labour Organization (ILO) Convention 107,[4] there has been recognition of the case for international protection of specific claims of indigenous groups.

As a matter of fact, the process of elaborating international standards for the protection of indigenous peoples is still in progress. A Draft Declaration on the Rights of Indigenous Peoples 1994[5] has been prepared and awaits approval by the United Nations. Before that, the ILO concluded a Convention on Indigenous and Tribal Peoples in 1989 which revises the 1957 Convention. These Conventions constitute limited evidence of the practice of the States parties on the subject of rights of indigenous groups.

But the number of States parties to these Conventions is relatively small.[6] The Conventions themselves are not of general application and may thus not be considered to be standard setting. It is therefore doubtful whether the standards contained in them as yet form part of general international law. At best, these Conventions evidence emerging standards concerning indigenous groups, and show that their protection is increasingly becoming a matter of international concern.

The United Nations Commission on Human Rights, which operates under the Economic and Social Council (ECOSOC) of the United Nations, has been involved in matters concerning the protection of indigenous groups through the United Nations Sub-Commission on the Prevention of Discrimination and Protection of Minorities since 1972.

In that year, the Sub-Commission commissioned Ambassador Jose Martinez Cobo as a special rapporteur to undertake a *Study of the Problem of the Discrimination Against Indigenous Populations*.[7] The Cobo report was completed in 1982. It made a series of recommendations relating to the definition, status and protection of indigenous groups generally. Its recommendations are obviously not law but the report bears a significant

[3] Brownlie, 'The Rights of Peoples in Modern International Law' in Crawford, *The Rights of Peoples*, n. 1 above, 2; *Treaties and Indigenous Peoples: The Robb Lectures* (F.M. Brookfield ed., Oxford, 1992).

[4] 328 U.N.T.S. 247.

[5] (1995) 34 I.L.M. 541.

[6] Convention 107 came into force on 26 June 1959. As of 1 January 1986, there were 26 States parties to it.

[7] E/C.N.4/Sub.2/1986/7.

evidential value relating to the need for the protection of indigenous groups and the nature of the claims involved.

There have also been numerous resolutions and declarations made in favour of international protection of indigenous groups at many international fora. The International Non-Governmental Organizations (N.G.O.) Conference on Indigenous Peoples of the Americas was held in 1977 at the United Nations in Geneva. A considerable number of N.G.O.s which have consultative status with the Economic and Social Council of the United Nations, and some Member States of the United Nations were in attendance.[8]

Recommendations of the Conference called for respect of traditional law and customs, unrestricted land rights of ownership of indigenous people, and control over natural resources located in traditional territories by indigenous people. Other Conferences of significance have been: the Inuit Circumpolar Conference held in Barrow, Alaska, in 1977 which, amongst a host of other recommendations, recommended recognition of the Inuit's (Eskimos) aboriginal territorial rights; the International N.G.O. Conference on Indigenous Peoples and the Land held at the United Nations in Geneva in 1981,[9] a follow up to that of 1977, which recommended self-determination of indigenous peoples, their right to develop and use their land resources, and to live in accordance with their values and philosophy.

International conferences have done much to heighten consciousness regarding claims made by indigenous groups and in generating international interest in the protection of such claims. Declarations and resolutions produced by such conferences have a certain moral and indirect legal value in pressing for international recognition of the claims of indigenous peoples. The Vienna Declaration called for the promotion and protection of the rights of indigenous people within international law in 1993 and called upon the Working Group to complete drafting the Declaration on Indigenous Peoples. These efforts, and the direct participation by indigenous groups in international fora, e.g. at the Vienna International Conference on Human Rights in 1993, will have a bearing on the development of international law in the context of indigenous peoples.

Existing forms of protection of indigenous groups within States by means of legislation constitutes evidence of the position of such States on the subject of the protection of indigenous groups. The content of such legislation is relevant to any assessment of the practice of States in formulating

[8] Some of these were the International Indian Treaty Council (I.I.T.C.), the World Council of Indigenous Peoples (W.C.I.P.), the South American Indian Council (C.I.S.A.), the Australian National Conference of Aborigines, the Indian Law Resource Centre (I.L.C.R.), and the Inuit Circumpolar Conference.

[9] U.N. Doc. E/C N.4/Sub.2/476/Add.5. 1981.

international rules of general application for the protection of indigenous groups.

Claims of indigenous groups revolve around the preservation of their special characteristics, culture and protection of their lifestyles. The point of significance concerns want of exclusive rights in respect of specific areas. This claim in large measure sets the issue of land rights and the concept of traditional ownership of a group, apart from the usual prescription of human rights on the basis of individual protection.[10]

In his illuminating *Study of the Problem of Discrimination Against Indigenous Populations*,[11] Cobo makes out the case for the importance to indigenous groups of exclusive ownership of traditional lands:

> It is essential to know and understand the deeply spiritual relationship between indigenous peoples and their land as basic to their existence as such and to all their beliefs, customs, traditions and culture.[12]

Cobo acknowledges that the special position of indigenous populations within the society of nation-States existing today derives from their historical rights to their land, as well as from their right to be different and to be considered different.[13]

But the quest for recognition of the special position of indigenous groups in relation to other population groups raises foremost the question of definition. The term 'indigenous people' has a political connotation which expresses the consciousness of a group whose characteristics are moulded by a common ancestry, language, culture, and ownership of traditional lands. It represents a demand for the international protection of these characteristics. Such protection has been sought by the International Labour Organization through Conventions 107 and 169 (Convention 169 superseded Convention 107). According to Convention 169,[14] indigenous peoples are distinct from other sections of the national community in their social, cultural, and economic conditions as well as status. The Convention calls for the status of indigenous groups to be regulated wholly, or partially, by their own customs or traditions, or by special laws or regulations.

The Convention regards as indigenous those groups which retain some, or all, of their own social, economic, cultural and political institutions on the basis of their descent from the populations which inhabited the country, or a geographical region to which the country belongs either at the time of conquest, colonization, or establishment of present State boundaries, and irrespective of their legal status. Self-identification on the part of certain groups 'as indigenous or tribal' is a fundamental criterion in determining whether certain groups should be beneficiaries of the standards contained

[10] Brownlie, 'The Rights of Peoples', n. 3 above, 3–4.
[11] E/CN.4/Sub.2/1986/7.
[12] E/CN4/Sub.2/1986/7/Add.4, p. 16.
[13] Ibid., at 29.
[14] Article 1(a)(b).

in it.[15] There is indeed a view held in some circles that indigenous people must be recognized according to their own perception and conception of themselves in relation to other groups.[16]

Cobo[17] has argued that the right of indigenous peoples themselves to define what and who is indigenous must be recognized as an expression of group consciousness. The rationale is that ethnic groups determine their own rules concerning membership, as well as the inclusion, or exclusion, of individuals that they may accept, or reject as members. Brownlie forcefully expresses the opinion that the heterogeneous terminology which has been used over the years—the references to 'nationalities', 'peoples', 'minorities' and 'indigenous populations'—involves essentially the same idea:

> Once a member of a people or community is expressing political claims in public discourse in Geneva, New York, Ottawa, or Canberra, and using the available stock of concepts so to do, it seems to me that the type of political consciousness involved is broadly the same. The external participation of culturally distinct groups in the political process is essentially the same as that of individual States in respect of the Law of Nations. By this I mean that in order to obtain recognition of the claim to cultural identity, or to statehood, the claimant must accept the terms of the dialogue. This may sound rather obvious but it is in this context that I want to make the point that the opposition which appears in the sources between the definition of indigenous populations 'by themselves' and 'by others' is a false dichotomy.[18]

Self-identification on the part of indigenous people is important as a means of pressing for recognition of their collective claims at the national and international level. It should not however condition the application of the standards aimed at protecting indigenous groups. The application of such standards must be based upon objective criteria.

One useful perspective in this regard is that in spite of the continuing doubt and difficulty over the definition of the word 'people', there is a core of reasonable certainty about it which may be derived from the principle of self-determination:

> This core consists in the right of the community which has a distinct character reflected in the institutions of government under which it lives. The concept of distinct character depends upon a number of criteria which may appear in combination. Race (or nationality) is one of the more important of the relevant criteria, but the concept of race can only be expressed scientifically in terms of more specific features, in which matters of culture, language, religion, and group psychology predominate.[19]

[15] Article 1(2).

[16] See, e.g., Alfredsson, 'Indigenous Populations, Protection', in Bernhardt (ed.), *Encyclopedia of Public International Law*, Instalment 8 (1985), 311.

[17] Cobo, *Conclusions, Proposals and Recommendations*, E/CN 4/Sub.2/1986/7/Add.4, at 28–9.

[18] Brownlie, 'Rights of Peoples', n. 3 above, 5–6.

[19] Ibid., at 5.

Adding a further dimension to the argument, Crawford[20] concisely states that there is no reason to suppose that what constitutes a people for the purpose of one right satisfies the requirements of another. Therefore, in his view, the definition of the concept 'people' could well be, and is likely to be, context dependent; it is objectionable to insist *a priori*, that a people is nothing but a whole population of existing States.

The views expressed above give a legal focus to the issues and approaches concerning efforts at defining indigenous people. In reference to indigenous groups, the term 'people' bears a strong legal connotation based upon the application of the principle of self-determination, and it presents a basis for determining the identity of indigenous groups, and for advancing their claims to protection within States.

Although definitions of a general nature have been proffered, international standards concerning the definition and protection of indigenous groups are still developing and no single definition commands general acceptance. Cobo[21] has suggested that for purposes of international action affecting their future existence:

> indigenous communities, peoples and nations are those which, having a historical continuity with pre-invasion and pre-colonial societies that developed on their territories, consider themselves distinct from other sectors of the societies now prevailing in those territories, or parts of them. They form at present non dominant sectors of society and are determined to preserve, develop and transmit to future generations their ancestral territories, and their ethnic identity, as the basis of their continued existence as peoples, in accordance with their cultural patterns, social institutions and legal systems.

The important elements in this definition include historical continuity and distinct character. In Cobo's treatment of the subject, both elements seem to overlap with historical continuity, which is seen as an extended period reaching into the present and encompassing the following: occupation of ancestral lands or part of them; common ancestry with the original occupants of the said lands; culture in general, or in specific manifestations such as religion, living under a tribal system, membership of an indigenous community, dress, means of livelihood and lifestyle; language; residence in certain parts of the country, or in certain regions of the world.

So far the Working Group on Indigenous People has not reached a consensus on the definition proposed by Cobo,[22] and the Draft Declaration fails to provide any definition of indigenous groups altogether. Although the definition proposed by Cobo places a certain amount of emphasis on the

[20] Crawford, *The Rights of Peoples*, n. 3 above, 169.

[21] *Study*, E/CN4/Sub.2/1986/7/Add.4, at 29.

[22] According to Kingsbury, *Indigenous Peoples in International Law* (D.Phil. Thesis, Oxford, 1990), at 24, several governments favour negotiation of definitions for specific purposes.

physical characteristics of groups, it has been argued, with some effect, that such physical characteristics do not condition but evidence the cultural distinctiveness of a group. The reasoning is that if the purely ethnic criteria are applied exclusively, many long-existing national identities, such as those of the USA, would be negated on academic grounds.[23]

Yet some sources tend to define indigenous people in terms of ethnic criteria. The *Encyclopedia of Public International Law*[24] describes indigenous people in general terms as the original inhabitants of a territory and who have been overcome, often outnumbered, but not assimilated by later settlers of different cultures and ethnic backgrounds who control national governments.

This conception may be applicable to limited cases such as the Australian Aborigines, American Indians, the Inuit or Eskimos, the Maoris in New Zealand, and the Lapps in Sweden. But it is not often the case that indigenous groups are outnumbered or constitute a minority. In the South American States of Bolivia and Guatemala, indigenous groups form the bulk of the population. The important point appears to be that indigenous groups exist and can clearly be identified within the specific context of their own setting by reference to their way of life, and certain characteristics which distinguish their identity or nationality from other groups or the rest of the population.[25]

In this chapter, discussion of the protection of indigenous groups is limited to restrictions on the movement and residence of persons within States. The chapter focuses on standards relating to restrictions which are created in order to protect collective claims of indigenous people to exclusive movement and residence on traditional territories. Such restrictions are seen as essential to the protection of claims of indigenous groups to exclusive occupation of their traditional lands.

Restrictions intended for the protection of indigenous groups may take the form of limitation of access by the general public to traditional territories inhabited by such groups. For example, section 81(b) of the Constitution of Kenya provides that restrictions may reasonably be imposed on persons generally or any class of interests for the protection or control of nomadic peoples.

Restrictions may also be used to exclude persons who do not belong to indigenous groups from moving and residing on parts of State territory which such groups traditionally occupy. Under section 130(3)(f) of the Constitution of Zimbabwe, restrictions may reasonably be imposed on the residence within Tribal Trust Land of persons who are not tribespeople for

[23] Brownlie, 'Rights of Peoples', n. 3 above, at 5. [24] Alfredsson, n. 16 above, 311.

[25] For a lengthy discussion of the definition of indigenous peoples, see Kingsbury, *Indigenous Peoples*, n. 22 above, ch. 1.

the protection of the interests of tribespeople or their well-being. Particular points of interest are tensions between indigenous groups' exclusive claims to reside on ancestral lands, and development strategies which include the relocation of indigenous people from their traditional lands for the purpose of land use and development planning.

2. EMERGING STANDARDS FOR THE PROTECTION OF INDIGENOUS GROUPS

Progress towards recognition of certain rights of groups of indigenous communities appears in instruments elaborated by the International Labour Organization. The measures undertaken by the ILO in this respect have at least been seen as an expression of growing international concern about widespread and harmful abusive practices against indigenous people.[26]

Thus in 1957, the ILO pioneered the adoption of the Convention on the Protection and Integration of Indigenous and Other Tribal People and Semi-tribal Populations.[27] This Convention set standards relating to special measures of protection of the institutions, persons, property and labour of tribal or semi-tribal populations, including minorities. Standards for the protection of these groups under this Convention were aimed at integrating and assimilating them into the rest of the population.

But the Convention failed to attract wide support, and Falk[28] explains that a fundamental deficiency of its approach was that it directly contradicted the definite preferences of indigenous people:

> Indigenous peoples increasingly resist integration and assimilation and seek above all to re-establish connections with their traditional lands and their traditional ways of life, so as to live with dignity and in a manner that reflects their own world view.

Consequently, the Indigenous and Tribal Peoples Convention was concluded in 1989[29] to establish new international standards to advance the international legal protection of indigenous and tribal peoples. The standards in this Convention are aimed at protecting the separate identity of indigenous people, their participation in issues of economic and cultural development which affect them; they also recognize their claims to traditional lands.

Article 3 of the Convention entitles indigenous and tribal peoples to the enjoyment of the full measure of human rights and fundamental freedoms without hindrance or discrimination. By establishing a link with general human rights standards, the Convention perhaps contemplates that its

[26] Falk, 'The Rights of Peoples', n. 1 above, 33.
[27] Convention 107, 328 U.N.T.S. 247.
[28] Falk, 'The Rights of Peoples', n. 1 above, 33.
[29] Convention 169.

framework of collective rights is not intended to dispense with individual rights. Article 3 further prohibits any use of force or coercion which violates either human rights and fundamental freedoms of indigenous and tribal peoples generally, or their collective rights under the Convention.

Special responsibility is placed upon governments to protect the rights of indigenous peoples, and to guarantee respect for their integrity.[30] This responsibility obliges governments to develop co-ordinated and systematic measures involving participation of the peoples concerned. The measures envisaged by the Convention include: non-discrimination against indigenous people regarding the benefits which arise from rights and opportunities that national laws and regulations grant to the rest of the population; promoting the full realization of the social, economic and cultural rights of indigenous and tribal people in matters of social and cultural identity, customs, traditions, and institutions; and assisting indigenous and tribal people to eliminate socio-economic gaps that may exist between indigenous groups and other members of the national community.

These measures entail application of a difference of treatment in order to safeguard persons belonging to tribal and indigenous groups, their institutions, culture, property, labour, and environment,[31] provided that any such special measures are in accordance with the freely expressed wishes of indigenous people, and do not prejudice their general rights of citizenship.

Standards contained in Convention 169 recognize the special importance of the connection between the cultural and spiritual values of indigenous people, and the lands or territories which they use or occupy. The Convention compels governments to respect this relationship, and to guarantee effectively indigenous peoples' rights to ownership and possession of such lands.[32]

As such, persons not belonging to indigenous groups are prohibited from taking advantage of either the customs of such peoples, or their lack of understanding of the laws securing their rights to ownership, possession or use of the land in question.[33] Provision is made in the Convention for consultation of indigenous peoples whenever consideration is being given to their capacity to alienate their lands or transmit their rights outside their own community.[34]

The Convention also protects rights of indigenous people to lands to which they traditionally have had access for their subsistence and traditional activities. Rights of nomadic peoples and shifting cultivators to have access to such lands are particularly singled out for protection, although such groups need not necessarily have exclusive occupation.[35] Although the standards set in this Convention are formative, they are evidenced by

[30] Ibid., Article 3. [31] Ibid., Article 4. [32] Ibid., Article 13, and Article 14(2).
[33] Ibid., Article 17(3). [34] Ibid., Article 17(2). [35] Ibid., Article 14(1).

certain municipal regimes. The study by Cobo[36] shows that in some countries, a systematic body of legal provisions has been established by means of laws, regulations, administrative and executive decisions which constitute a legal regime applicable to the indigenous populations of such countries.

Amongst the countries with such constitutional regimes are Nicaragua, Paraguay, Venezuela, the Philippines, and Canada.[37] In practice, special measures designed for the protection of the collective interests of indigenous groups involve restrictions on internal residence and movement which are reinforced by penalties for unlawful entry on particular lands.[38]

3. LEGALITY OF RESTRICTIONS CONCERNING THE PROTECTION OF INDIGENOUS PEOPLES

Restrictions which are imposed for the protection of indigenous people touch upon the application of the principle of non-discrimination and equality of treatment in the sense of positive measures. Under current human rights standards, the principle of non-discrimination is central to the protection of indigenous groups in addition to specific standards being advocated towards that end.

Non-discrimination entitles indigenous groups to the equal protection of the law and to the enjoyment of human rights generally. Equality of treatment involves special measures designed not only to protect special interests of indigenous groups but also to advance their well-being to relatively the same level as that attained by the rest of the population. Such special measures usually take the form of restrictions which appear to place practical constraints upon the movement and residence of non-indigenous persons in areas inhabited by indigenous groups. But the pertinent question is whether the restriction has legal justification in the sense of non-discrimination.

This constituted the substantial issue in the Australian case of *Gerhardy v Brown*.[39] The case arose from a complaint made under the Racial Discrimination Act of the Commonwealth of Australia 1975. The Racial Discrimination Act made specific adoption for application within Australia of the standards contained in the Convention on the Elimination of All Forms of Racial Discrimination 1965. The Act prescribed as unlawful any act involving racial discrimination and which had the purpose or the effect of

[36] E/CN 4/Sub.2/1986/7/Add.4, p. 5.

[37] Vol. II, EC/N.4/Sub.2/1986/7/Add. 1, pp. 96–119, 124.

[38] For example, the Lands Act of Southern Australia 1981, s. 18; the Tribal Trust Land Act of Zimbabwe, s. 14(1); and the Indigenous and Tribal Peoples' Convention calls for adequate penalties to be established by law for unauthorized intrusion and use of indigenous lands, and also requires of governments to take measures to prevent such offence.

[39] (1985) 57 A.L.R. 472.

impairing the enjoyment of human rights on an equal footing in any aspect of public life.[40] Among such rights included in the Act was that of movement and residence within States under Article 5(d)(i) of the Convention on the Elimination of All Forms of Racial Discrimination.

However, the Act excluded from the scope of discrimination certain provisions relating to special measures permitted under the Convention. According to the Convention, these measures had to have the sole purpose of securing adequate advancement of certain racial groups in order to secure their equal enjoyment of human rights. Provided that, under terms set by the Convention, such special measures did not lead to the maintenance of separate rights for different racial groups, and that those measures were not continued after the objectives for which they were taken had been achieved.[41]

In *Gerhardy v Brown*, such special measures largely formed the subject-matter of the Pitjatjatjara Lands Act of Southern Australia 1981. The Act vested title to a large area of land in the North-West of South Australia in the Pitjantjatjara aboriginal peoples on grounds of traditional ownership.[42] The Pitjantjatjara were defined by the Act as persons who were members of the Pitjatjatjara, Yungkutatjara or Ngaanatjara people, and traditional owners of land.

Section 18 of the Act gave the Pitjantjatjara unrestricted right of access to the lands which comprised a declared Aboriginal Reserve. Subject to some exceptions, a non-Pitjantjatjara who entered the lands without permission of the Pitjantjatjara body corporate was guilty of an offence in terms of section 19(1) of the Act. This provision prohibited non-Pitjantjatjaras from entering freely the lands which were set aside for the exclusive occupation of the Pitjantjatjara people. The body corporate was itself constituted under the Act as 'Anangu Pitjantjatjaraku' which represented the Pitjantjatjara people.

The respondent, Robert Brown, was himself an aboriginal person whose tribal origins were apparently in New South Wales and was not a member of any of the groups of people who were permitted to reside on the lands stipulated by the Act. As no formal permission had been granted for him to enter the lands, he was charged on the complaint of the appellant that he committed a breach of section 19(1) of the Act.

Before the High Court of Australia, the case rested on the legality of the Land Act itself. It raised the issue whether the Act was a special measure under the provisions of the Racial Discrimination Act of Australia. In justifying the Act as a special measure the court gave weight to the concept

[40] Racial Discrimination Act of 1975, s. 9(1).

[41] Convention on the Elimination of All Forms of Racial Discrimination of 1965, Article 1(4).

[42] Pitjantjatjara Lands Act, ss. 5, 15.

of traditional ownership of land. It stated the view that the right of access to traditional lands under section 18 of the Act was enjoyed by persons of the aboriginal race, and not by persons of any other race. No person could enjoy that right unless he or she was a traditional owner of a part of the lands in question. Hence even if the respondent was himself an Aborigine, he was not a traditional owner of the Pitjantjatjara lands and therefore had no right of access to these lands.

Chief Justice Gibbs[43] commented on the problems which arise from such restrictions as follows:

> A person who enjoys a right under S.18 of the Act enjoys it without any restrictions—that is to say, of course, any restriction imposed by the Act itself; other laws may limit the right. Moreover, the qualification for enjoying the right—traditional ownership—is itself based on racial origin. Recourse to the notion of traditional ownership may readily be had to the most obnoxious discrimination. On one hand, members of a particular race may be confined to one area, not, it may be said, because of their race, but because it is their traditional homeland; on the other hand, the right to own land may be conferred only on members of a favoured race, not it may be said, because they belong to that race, but because they are traditional owners.

The limitation of access to lands occupied by the Pitjantjatjara under section 19 of the Act was held by the court to be a special measure of protection. According to the court, the object of the Land Act was to give rights to the lands to a group of associated peoples who traditionally owned various parts of them. Importance was attached in the Act to protecting the interests of the traditional owners, and preserving Pitjantjatjara traditions and culture:

> The legislature no doubt acted on the view that to enable the Pitjantjatjara to live on the land in accordance with their traditions and customs and to maintain their relationship to the land, which is a relationship quite different from that which persons of European descent are accustomed, it is necessary not only that they should own the land but also that they should have full control of access to it.[44]

The court seemed to concede that the Land Act was discriminatory by reference to race, colour, or origin and that the Act amounted to an impairment of internal movement,[45] but then proceeded to find that the Act was justified as a special measure.

The decision in *Gerhardy v Brown* may be criticized for this faulty approach. The necessary approach would have been for the court to determine that the Land Act was not discriminatory in the first place because it had a reasonable and legitimate objective in protecting common aboriginal ownership of land as well as preserving the way of life of the Pitjantjatjara.

43 *Gerhardy v. Brown*, n. 39 above, at 481.
44 Ibid., at 483; also per Justice Mason at 497.
45 Per Justice Mason at 496.

Nevertheless, the position taken by the court concerning the justification of restrictions limiting general movement and residence on indigenous lands is basically correct within meaning of the principle of non-discrimination.

In the context of the protection of indigenous groups, the objective of restrictions is to provide positive special measures of protection by seeking to limit or exclude general movement and residence on traditional territory occupied by indigenous groups as a means of protecting their title to traditional lands and preserving their way of life. For instance, in *Gerhardy v Brown*, Justice Mason saw the Land Act as a legislative measure which sought to convert the traditional land ownership of the Pitjantjatjara people into a modern legal framework approximating closely as may be to the central feature of traditional aboriginal ownership.

The claim of traditional ownership is inseparable from the objective of preserving indigenous lifestyles and the attainment of effective and genuine equality between indigenous groups and the rest of the population. Thus, traditional ownership, preservation of indigenous ways of life, and equality of treatment of indigenous groups on the basis of non-discrimination represent the main candidates for recognition as collective or group rights of indigenous people.

Equality of treatment under non-discrimination provides a firm legal basis of protecting indigenous groups under current human rights standards. Because the principle of non-discrimination has received recognition as being of general application under customary international law, as well as belonging to the category of obligations *erga omnes* in matters of race, it is applicable generally to cases of positive measures, including those relating to group rights. On this basis, it may be argued that legislative measures designed within State territory to restore ownership of traditional lands to indigenous groups, and to preserve their characteristics or ways of life, are reasonable and justifiable as an aspect of equality of treatment under the principle of non-discrimination.

Within this context, restrictions which prohibit general movement and residence on territory occupied by indigenous groups may be considered permissible and reasonably justified. It is reasonable to make the assessment that restrictions of this kind are necessary to protect collective ownership of traditional lands with respect to specific territories inhabited by indigenous groups. In addition, such restrictions may be used similarly to establish forms of autonomy for indigenous groups where this is desirable as a matter of protection and self-determination within the State.[46]

However, there are difficult problems connected with restrictions which exclude general movement and residence within State territory in order to protect collective rights of indigenous groups. The first is that restrictions

[46] Note for instance the claims for autonomy presented by the Kurds in the northern territory of Iraq and the controversial safe havens created for the protection of the Kurds.

of this kind can maintain rigid constraints upon general movement and residence within the State and upon the desire of members of indigenous groups who wish to assimilate. The element of choice must, therefore, be present.

As Justice Brennan[47] remarked:

> The purpose of securing advancement for a racial group is not established by showing that the branch of government or the person who takes the measure does so for the purpose of conferring what it or he regards as the benefit of the group if the group does not seek or wish to have that benefit. The wishes of the beneficiaries for the measure are of great importance (perhaps essential too) in determining whether a measure is taken for the purpose of securing their advancement. The dignity of the beneficiaries is impaired and they are not advanced by having an unwanted material foisted upon them. An aboriginal community without a home is advanced by granting them title to the land they wish to have as a home. Such a grant may satisfy the demand for land rights. But an aboriginal community would not be advanced by granting them title to land in which they would be confined against their wishes. Such a grant would be a step towards apartheid. Even if the promoters of the measure had the purpose of promoting the interests of the residents of that land, the measure would deny the residents' human rights and fundamental freedoms.

It would appear that, from the point of formal equality, indigenous persons must be entitled to the enjoyment of all rights, including movement and residence within the State, which are exercised by the rest of the population. Conversely, there must be careful legislative means of regulation of movement in general as opposed to prohibition of entry or access to indigenous lands. This regulation of movement may be administered by indigenous people themselves for purposes of allowing visits, peaceful association, or entry connected with the welfare of indigenous groups.

The second problem relates to the conflict of collective and individual rights within the set up of an indigenous group. Rights of an indigenous group which may clash with rights of individual members of the group include restriction of access to traditional lands as a matter of control, and the collective ownership of traditional lands, particularly in relation to management and use of the lands for the general interest of the group. Unrestricted access to traditional lands may be open to an indigenous group collectively as well as to its individual members. A representative body of the group or individuals belonging to it may enforce or control access by non-members to the lands. But a member of the group should obviously be precluded from granting access to associates who are not members of the group without the consent of the group.

For example, in *Gerhardy v Brown*[48] it was acknowledged to be true that section 19, in requiring a non Pitjantjatjara to apply to Anangu Pitjantjat-

[47] Per Justice Brennan, *Gerhardy v Brown*, n. 39 above, at 521.

[48] Per Justice Brennan at 507; see also at 520.

jaraku or its delegate for permission to enter and in requiring the permission to be written, precludes, perhaps harshly, an individual Pitjantjatjara from inviting a non-Pitjantjatjara onto the land. Individual convenience has given way to group protection. It follows, too, then that an individual member of an indigenous group is prohibited from alienating a portion of traditional territory to a non-member of the group even if the individual be a traditional owner of such land. The criterion of traditional ownership, namely that traditional owners must be indigenous persons, ultimately operates to protect the collective interests of the group in relation to collective ownership and land use. It also serves to give primacy to the wishes or opinions of indigenous people in relation to their traditional affiliation with land.

The main issue to be considered in this case is whether the collective interests of the group should override those of individual members. In general terms, collective rights must naturally imply that the rights of individuals in a given context are subordinate. Moreover, it has been said that advocates of collective rights conceive such rights as a basis for the fulfilment of individual rights and that accordingly, a collective right accorded a high priority may be construed as superior to an individual right which is deemed inconsistent with the implementation of the collective right.[49]

Against this proposition, Shachter put forward the argument that collective rights may turn human rights upside down in that the collectivity is recognized as having claims on the individual, and the individual as having obligations to the State or other collective entity.[50] As for groups of minorities and indigenous people, Shachter notes that these have both individual and collective rights, and calls for a process of accommodation of individual and collective rights as in other cases of competing rights.

However, in the context of the collective rights of groups, the matter goes beyond the process of accommodation of rights. It is doubtful whether certain collective rights concerning group identity and traditional land ownership can be protected by the accommodation of rights on the basis of current individual prescriptions of human rights in international law.

In any case, the concept of group rights represents a desire to reinforce and advance the existing concepts of human rights and is said not to be simply a re-run of notions of human rights.[51] Collective rights of indigenous groups which relate to preserving their lifestyle and ownership of traditional lands have a role in preserving their existence as such. Recognition of these rights may consequently entail a fair erosion of certain rights of individual members of the group if this is essential to fulfilling and

[49] Schachter, 'General Course in Public International Law' (1982) V *Recueil* 9–376.
[50] Ibid. [51] See Brownlie, 'The Rights of Peoples', n. 3 above, 11.

securing the group's uninterrupted enjoyment of the use and ownership of the lands as a collective entity.

For instance, the right of an individual member of an indigenous group to unrestricted alienation of traditional lands must be subject to the group's interest of common ownership of the land because this has to do with the means of existence of the group as a whole. Where group rights are concerned, the position of the individual has to be viewed very much in the light of the group to which the individual belongs. For it is usually the case in the context of group rights that the position and welfare of the individual depend on the well-being and advancement of the group itself.[52] Within the group, however, individual rights, such as non-discrimination, must apply.

There is a further clash of interests involving the protection of indigenous groups which goes beyond the group and its individual members. It concerns a broad conflict of interests between the group itself and society at large. This conflict relates to the protection of the common ownership of traditional lands by exclusion of general entry in the interest of the group, and the public requirements of land use and planning which sometimes lead to the forcible relocation of indigenous groups from their traditional lands to other areas within State territory. It is to this issue that the discussion now turns.

4. FORCED MOVEMENT OR RELOCATION OF INDIGENOUS GROUPS

Groups of indigenous people are vulnerable to forcible relocation from strategically significant traditional lands as a consequence of land use and development planning in many parts of the world, particularly in developing countries.[53] Acts of forcible relocation generally involve restriction of movement and choice of residence, denial of traditional ownership of land, the preservation of group identity which is usually connected with traditional lands, and denial of access to the resources of regions traditionally inhabited by indigenous groups.[54] Two cases of relocation are examined

[52] On the general question of the individual and community rights, see Brownlie, *Principles of Public International Law*, 5th edn. (Oxford, 1998), 605.

[53] For example, the Federal Government of Rhodesia in 1957 forcibly relocated indigenous groups belonging to the Tonga communities residing along the Gwembe Valley in Zambia (then Northern Rhodesia) in order to pave the way for the construction of the Kariba dam. A section of this community was again moved from their lands in Sinazongwe because the lands were required for wheat production; other examples include the removal of Indians from the Amazons in Equador; the relocation of Indians in North Western Brazil during construction of the Polonoroeste hydro-electric scheme; the displacement of around 41,000 people in India during implementation of projects under the Seventh Five-year Plan in 1984.

[54] For example s. 81(d) of the Kenyan Constitution states that restrictions on movement and residence include restrictions on the use of land.

below, namely the relocation of Miskito Indians in Nicaragua, and the Barabaig nomads in Tanzania.

(i) Relocation of Miskito Indians

The Miskito Indians in Nicaragua have traditionally inhabited the Atlantic coast in the Eastern region of Nicaragua which, since 1894, has been administratively organized as the Department of Zelaya. In the period between 1880 and 1935, legal arrangements were made concerning, amongst other things, restitution and recognition of legal personality of Miskitos. A decree was passed in early 1893 which provided for the Miskito Indians to remain under the protection of the Republic of Nicaragua and that all income derived from the coast would be invested for their benefit.[55]

Upon coming to power in Nicaragua, the Sandinista Government adopted a positive policy towards the Miskitos and initiated moves intended for their internal self-determination.[56] However, in late 1981, the Sandinista Government decided to relocate forcibly the Miskitos from the Coco river region to five settlements called the Tasba Pri in Miskito. The settlements were situated approximately 60 miles from the border with Honduras.[57]

The immediate reason advanced by the Sandinistas for the forcible evacuation of the Miskitos was based on military necessity due to a state of emergency.[58] Concentrated on both sides of the border between neighbouring Nicaragua and Honduras, the community of Miskitos occupied a strategic geo-political position. Hostile relations developed between Nicaragua and Honduras when the Contras—armed bands and remnants of the deposed Somoza Government's National Guard opposed to the Sandinista Government—established military training camps in Honduras on the left bank of the Coco river occupied by Miskitos.

It was obvious that the Sandinistas suspected the Miskitos of acting in collusion with the Contras in destabilizing Nicaragua. But apart from these reasons of military necessity, the matter of the forced resettlement of the Miskitos was complicated by another factor. The Sandinista Government had in fact previously planned to relocate the Miskitos from the banks of the Coco river to what it considered more fertile and secure lands. Among other things, this decision was based on considerations relating to the frequent flooding of the villages on the river banks. According to the Government, because of the rising of the Coco river, sufficient food or food

[55] Cobo, *Study*, n. 21 above, 90.

[56] See *Declaration of Principles of the Popular Sandinista Revolution in regard to the Indigenous Communities of the Atlantic Coast* 1980; Ortiz, *Indians of the Americas: Human Rights and Self-Determination* (London, 1984), 195–235.

[57] These settlements were named Wasminona, Sahasa, Sumubila, Truslaya, and Columbus.

[58] See above, Chapter 4.

of sufficient nutritional value could not be produced in this area. Had it not been for the military necessity which pre-empted it, the resettlement process was planned to be carried out in stages, beginning with persuading the Miskitos to resettle.

A government publication titled 'Tasba Pri' explained the reasons which altogether led the Sandinista Government to consider relocating the Miskitos:

> The Tasba Pri program is not something new and improvised. It was immediately preceded by the feasibility study undertaken by the Revolutionary Government through its Nicaragua Institute of the Atlantic Coast (INNCA) in November of 1980, to improve and lend dignity to the lives of the Miskitos inhabiting the Nicaraguan side of the Coco River. This resettlement will safeguard the Miskito population from the attacks of counter revolutionary bands, and ensures protection of their principal human rights: the right to work in peace. The resettlements will also solve the historic problems of the inhabitants, which are a subsistence agriculture, lack of fertile lands, inaccessibility of the region and consequent difficulties for transporting inputs and obtaining state services, and the floods which annually cause serious damage to housing and crops.

Within the settlements, the Miskitos were organized in family and neighbourhood units which the Indian peoples were said to be accustomed to, as a way of maintaining their social structures.

In March 1982, a complaint concerning 'Violations of Indian Human Rights in the East Coast of Nicaragua' was brought before the Inter-American Commission for Human Rights. The Commission was strict in finding a limited justification for the forcible relocation of the Miskitos due to reasons of military necessity.[59] In its view, the plan to relocate voluntarily the Coco river populations in order to improve and lend dignity to their living conditions would have been justifiable only if that move had been voluntary.

Consequently, the Commission stated that the Miskitos who chose not to remain in Tasba Pri once the emergency was over would have to return to the Coco river region. In the opinion of the Commission, to impede their return directly or indirectly would imply that the resettlement arising from the compulsory relocation was permanent. This would be in violation of the right to movement and residence set forth in the American Convention on Human Rights.

The Commission went on to say that the Nicaraguan Government should expressly declare that the Tasba Pri project may only be carried out with the Miskitos who voluntarily chose to remain there. In addition, the Commission required of the Government to declare that it would assist in

[59] This issue, and the views of the Commission thereon, will be considered below in Chapter 7, pp. 139–141.

resettling other Miskitos who wished to return to the Coco river region and grant them adequate compensation for the loss of their property.

Reference was made in this respect to the general principles applicable to situations of relocation of populations. According to the Commission, the preponderant doctrine is that massive relocation of population groups may be juridically valid if done with the consent of the population involved.

On this basis the Commission stipulated that the large majority of population relocations for reasons of economic development have taken place after negotiations with the populace concerned, and with assurances of adequate compensation. It seemed to acknowledge a possible exception to the application of this principle of some cases involving the relocation of Indians, which it said were nevertheless subject to criticism. Attention was drawn by the Commission to the problems which relocated Indian populations encounter in view of their special ties with their original lands:

> In the Indian's complex scheme of values, what gives meaning to life is its intrinsic connection with their land, their livestock, their plantations, their cemeteries, their religion and a complex weave of other elements that can combine to infuse the territory with a deep spiritual meaning. In that culture, a sense of value is closely tied to one's place of origin. For that reason, it is important that the international community seek to avoid, if possible, disturbances of Indian populations.[60]

The pronouncements of the Commission in relation to consent as the basis of relocation were based upon a resolution of the Institute of International Law in 1952[61] according to which relocations may be legal only if they are voluntary. Application of this principle by the Commission shows that it is a general principle of international law.

Thus the requirement of consent is seen as a safeguard against forcible relocation. But consent alone, even with guarantees of compensation, may not be adequate to safeguard against forced removals of population groups. It is plausible to argue that consent in relation to relocation should be seen in the light of, or in addition to, human rights standards concerning freedom of movement and choice of residence within States.

The Commission adverted to a possible violation of these standards in the case of the relocation of Miskito Indians, but it did not elaborate the point further. However, it need not have done so once it found that reasons of military necessity justified the relocation in accordance with the principle of derogation. But the Commission did examine the justification of the Tasba Pri plan to relocate the Miskitos as an issue prior to that of military necessity. It would have been pertinent for the Commission to consider whether the original plan to relocate the Miskitos was permissible on

[60] IACHR, *Report on the Situation of Human Rights of a Segment of the Nicaraguan Population of Miskito Origin* (DEA/Ser./V/II.62, doc. 26, 1984), 47–8.

[61] (1952) 44/2 *Annuaire* 138.

general grounds stipulated by the standards concerning restrictions on freedom of movement and choice of residence within States.

The relocation of the Miskitos as previously envisaged in the Tasba Pri could not have been justified on these standards. No legislation had been passed or even proposed to effect the resettlement, and the proposed ground for resettlement, namely economic development, is not recognized or included in the relevant standards as a category upon which internal movement and residence may be restricted. Therefore the original design to relocate the Miskitos on grounds specified by the Tasba Pri programme would have been impermissible under the international standards concerning restrictions on the movement and residence of people within States.

Although these standards are relevant to cases of relocation, there is doubt as to whether they can be used effectively to check the implementation of relocations enforced under specific national legislation such as the Indian Statute[62] in Brazil. This statute provides that the removal of a tribal group shall only be resorted to when it is quite impossible or inadvisable to allow it to remain in the area inhabited by it, in which case the native community, on removal, shall be assigned an area equivalent to the former one. The standards applicable to restrictions on internal movement and residence cannot in all cases provide an absolute guarantee against relocation. As the Cobo report[63] observes, guarantees proclaimed even in constitutions, of the possession by indigenous communities of their lands, are rendered inoperative by stipulations allowing intervention by the public authorities in their areas which provide for the removal of entire communities on specified grounds that are broadly defined.

One weakness in the standards under consideration is apparent. A State which restricts movement and residence whether by relocation or otherwise by means of legislation stipulating grounds corresponding to those contained in international law *prima facie* conforms to international standards. In such circumstances, the main consideration would be whether the restriction is reasonable and proportionate to the objective for which it is sought.

A synthesis of applicable standards, i.e. those relating to permissible restrictions on movement and residence, and the requirement of the consent of the affected group as a basis of protection against forced resettlement is proposed. In assessing whether restriction of movement and residence by forced resettlement is reasonable and legitimate, the element of consent on the part of the population concerned must be a relevant factor to take into account.

Consent on the part of the affected population to relocate may be taken as *prima facie* evidence of the reasonableness and legitimacy of the

[62] Law No. 6001 of 1973, Article 20(3). [63] E/CN.4/Sub.2/1986/7/Add.4, p. 16.

objective to resettle it. Conversely, absence of such consent may be an important indication of the likelihood that the measure of relocation may be unreasonable and illegitimate. Consent nevertheless remains a separate principle which operates to guarantee the protection of indigenous groups against forced relocation. A State which invokes measures involving resettlement must bear the burden of showing that the group concerned consented to be resettled.

The ILO Conventions express an obligation incumbent upon States to pay adequate compensation as a consequence of relocation.[64] This obligation, like the principle of consent, must rank in status as a general principle of law. It was applied by the Inter-American Commission on Human Rights with respect to the relocation of Miskitos independently of any treaty basis.

In the case concerning the relocation of Miskitos, the Nicaraguan Government claimed that it had compensated the relocated Miskitos by giving them land, homes, seeds, fertilizers, and farm tools in their resettlements, as well as medical attention without charge. The Commission seemed to imply that such a framework would not constitute adequate compensation.

It required of the Nicaraguan Government to declare that it would assist in resettling other Miskitos who wished to return to the Coco river region and grant them adequate compensation for the loss of their property.[65] So far as the Commission was concerned, the provision of an alternative social framework in Tasba Pri was neither requested nor accepted by the Miskitos. The trend set by the ILO Conventions tends to lay a duty on the part of the State to consult with indigenous people regarding measures which affect them.[66] Present indications are that the development of future standards as evidenced by the United Nations Draft Declaration on Indigenous People[67] are likely to place preference on consultation rather than consent in relation to large-scale projects affecting indigenous people.

It has been suggested that the requirement of consultation, participation, and self-representation of indigenous peoples as well as certain forms of autonomy of indigenous peoples, are emerging as general principles supported by international and municipal practice.[68] With respect to restrictions affecting internal movement and residence, consultation of indigenous people, and their participation in measures relating to their relocation, may

[64] Convention 169, Article 16(5); Convention 107, Article 12(3).

[65] For discussion of the application of the duty to pay compensation in cases of relocation, see Kingsbury, *Indigenous Peoples*, pp. 158–62.

[66] See e.g. Art. 6 of Convention 109.

[67] E/CN.4/Sub.2/1989, Annex II, Principle 17.

[68] Kingsbury, *Indigenous Peoples*, n. 22 above, 161.

be used as evidence in assessing the reasonableness and the legitimacy of the restriction.

(ii) Relocation of the Barabaig Group

The Barabaig are a pastoral group of more than 30,000 people in Tanzania. They have inhabited the rich plains of land around Mount Hanag in central Tanzania for more than 150 years. Their economic activity and lifestyle is based on cattle rearing. They have employed a complex system of land grazing rotation in the semi-arid lands of Hanang district in order to maximize the use of available vegetation in separate areas of the district and at different times throughout the year.

Because of their pastoral pattern of life, the Barabaig have been unfairly regarded as a 'backward' people incapable of adjusting to Tanzania's modern way of life. In 1969 their traditional land was alienated for a large-scale government agricultural scheme called the Tanzania Canada Wheat Project. This project was financed by the Canadian International Development Agency (CIDA) (which has since contracted out!) and administered by the National Agricultural and Food Corporation of Tanzania. An area of 70,000 acres was alienated originally and an additional 30,000 acres were alienated in 1979, altogether without compensation.

The expropriation of the Barabaig's traditional land was accompanied by crude methods of general harassment, killing of their cattle, setting their homes on fire, and desecrating their sacred objects and sites, including graves which have a unique cultural value to the Barabaig.[69] The relocation was undertaken pursuant to the provisions of the Land Acquisition Act 1967. Section 4(2) of this Act states that:

> Where the President is satisfied that a corporation requires any land for the purposes of construction of any work which in his opinion would be of public utility or in the public interest or in the interest of the national economy, he may, with the approval, to be signified by resolution, of the National Assembly and by order pub-

[69] See 'Tanzania: Executive Order Denies Land Rights; Barabaig Suffer Beatings, Arson and Criminal Charges', *News From Africa Watch*, 12 March 1990. In an open letter four elders have appealed on behalf of the entire Barabaig as follows: 'Widespread human rights abuses are associated with the conduct of the project. When moving us NAFCO have sometimes burnt us out of our homes without warning. In this way some people have lost all their possessions, including some food reserves. At other times they have ploughed around the homestead making it impossible for us to come and go freely. When attempting to reach pasture, water or salt by following traditional routes across the farms we are deemed "trespassers" and subjected to beatings and fines. We find it hard to resist this harassment as NAFCO call on the police and militia to enforce their will on us. Many of the graves of our elders have been ploughed up and are no longer recognisable. These sacred sites are very important to us as places of worship. It is there that we make offerings and call on God's blessings through the medium of our ancestors. This desecration is tantamount to the deliberate destruction of a church and graveyard in a Christian community in Canada'.

lished in the gazette, declare the purpose for which such land is required to be a public purpose and upon such order being made such purpose shall be deemed to be a public purpose for the purposes of the Act.

The Barabaig have claimed that their traditional lands must be restored to their possession. Their claim is based on the customary right of occupancy and control of their traditional lands.[70] They have argued that:

because of the continuing abuses of our rights, and the fact that the broader question of whether we have customary title to the land we occupied is still unresolved, we have decided to go back to the Courts. We contend that NAFCO failed to adhere to the due process of law in acquiring this land and are thus trespassing on the extra 30,000 acres. We are demanding fair compensation for the loss of the land, the destruction of our homes and desecration of our graves. We want restoration of traditional rights of way that will allow us to reach grazing, water and salt as before. We want to establish once and for all that indigenous pastoral communities have customary rights to the land they occupy so that their future livelihoods may be protected by the law of the land.[71]

In the case of *Mulbadaw Village Council and 67 Others v National Agricultural and Food Corporation*[72] the plaintiffs challenged the alienation of their lands to NAFCO in the High Court of Tanzania. Their argument was that they were lawful owners of the land in issue.

Mulbadaw Village Council was registered and incorporated as a village under the Villages and Ujamaa Villages Act 1975. The defendant did not deny that it entered into and still occupied land at Mulbadaw. It however pleaded that it had been carrying out a lawful Tanzanian national wheat project in an area identified by the Tanzanian Government for that purpose. It argued that it was in lawful occupation of the land in issue and the Land Acquisition Act was not applicable to land held by peasants under customary land tenure, except formal rights of occupancy.

This argument failed to persuade the High Court which noted that the definition of rights of occupancy under the Land Ordinance Act 1967 included titles of peasants holding land under customary tenure. In the opinion of the court, the Village Council were in lawful possession and control of the land in question because they had been in occupation for a considerable time before NAFCO expanded its activities. Accordingly, the plaintiffs had customary tenancies or deemed rights of occupancy which could not be extinguished or superseded except by due operation of law.

The court held that the provisions of the Land Acquisition Act were not

[70] Section 17 of the Land Acquisition Act provides that where any question arises respecting title to any land the party in possession shall be deemed to be lawfully entitled to such land unless the contrary is shown to the satisfaction of the court.

[71] *News From Africa Watch.*

[72] High Court of Tanzania, Civil Case No. 10 of 1981.

duly observed, and that where someone was in lawful occupation of land, no valid right of occupancy could be offered to anyone else over the same land unless the provisions of the Land Acquisition Act had been complied with. This decision rested on section 17 of the Land Acquisition Act which provides that where any question arose concerning title to any land, the party in possession shall be entitled to such land unless the contrary was shown to the satisfaction of the court. On this basis the court determined that NAFCO's entry upon the lands in dispute was illegal.

The defendants lodged an appeal against this decision.[73] The Court of Appeal held that the Mulbadaw Village Council had failed to establish that it was in occupation of, or owned, the lands in question since its registration and incorporation in 1977. In the opinion of the Court of Appeal, if the villagers who had testified before the High Court had established that as natives they had occupancy by virtue of customary tenancies then the view of the High Court that such villagers could only be evicted under the provisions of the Land Acquisition Act would have been sound.

The Court of Appeal erred in restricting claims of ownership or possession of the land in question to the period after 1977 when the Village Council was registered. It conveniently ignored the fact that the villagers of Mulbadaw were in occupation of the contested land before 1977, and thus avoided examining the question of title to those lands before 1977 as well as that of successor to title after 1977. It was not necessary for the plaintiffs to prove that they were natives,[74] and in the circumstances the court should either have taken judicial notice of that fact, or ascertained that the plaintiffs were Tanzanian citizens. The issue remained whether the provisions of the Land Acquisition Act concerning alienation of land (section 4(?) in particular) had been followed. If, as was the case, such provisions were not complied with, then the plaintiffs remained the lawful owners of the land in issue under section 17 of the Land Acquisition Act, notwithstanding the registration and incorporation of Mulbadaw Village in 1977.

Later in 1986, 20 villagers in the case of *Lagwen Ifray and 19 Others v Nangwa Village Council*[75] brought an action in the High Court against the village council on grounds of unlawful removal from their traditional lands. The High Court determined that the lands in question had been expropriated illegally.

Another 105 similar cases were pending before the High Court. Consequently the Tanzanian Government later issued an order in 1987 to

[73] *National Agricultural and Food Corporation and Mulbadaw Village Council and Others*, Court of Appeal, Civil Appeal No. 3 of 1985.

[74] Under an amendment to the Land Ordinance Act No. 28 of 1970, a native 'means any person who is a citizen of the United Republic and who is not of European or Asiatic Origin or descent'.

[75] Civil Case No. 4 of 1982.

extinguish the customary rights of the Barabaig villagers who were pursuing these cases. It was to take similar action again in 1989 when applications were filed which sought to secure compensation for the Barabaig with respect to the original 70,000 acres of Barabaig traditional land, and to dispute title of NAFCO to the additional 30,000 acres it subsequently alienated.[76]

The Tanzanian Government forestalled this action by issuing an official notice extinguishing customary rights of the Barabaig in lands occupied by NAFCO.[77] The notice was applied retrospectively in that it was presented as an amendment to the Order of 1987. Its effect was to take away the claims of the Barabaig to their traditional lands from as far back as 1987.

The relocation of the Barabaig did not conform to international standards concerning resettlement. From the point of view of general standards, the element of consent and the emergent requirements of consultation, and the participation of the Barabaig in the decision to relocate them, are clearly absent. Within Africa, regional standards contained in the African Charter of Human and People's Rights give recognition to people's rights as opposed to States. Article 21(1) of the Charter provides that all peoples shall freely dispose of their wealth and natural resources. It proposes a strict standard by stating that in no case shall a people be deprived of this right. In the framework of the Charter, the Barabaig are a 'people' on account of a distinct character and way of life, and would be entitled to dispose of their wealth and natural resources freely without being coerced to do so.

In addition, there is a failure by the Tanzanian Government to provide compensation as a remedy for loss of land rights or other property arising from resettlement, contrary to Article 21(2) of the African Charter. This provision requires that in case of spoliation, the dispossessed people shall have the right to lawful recovery of its property as well as to an adequate compensation.

This means that a dispossessed people are not only entitled to adequate compensation but also to recovery of their property by lawful means where spoliation has taken place. As such, the Barabaig would have a right to receive compensation, to recovery of their property, and are entitled to resort to lawful means in order to recover their property.

There is also the question of restriction of the movement and residence of Barabaig by virtue of forced relocation. Such a restriction seems to have been effected by means of legislation authorizing compulsory acquisition of property. However, the ground on which the restriction operates, i.e., agricultural development, does not constitute a permissible ground for limiting movement and choice of place of residence under general

[76] These applications were brought by the Legal Aid Committee at the University of Dar es Salaam.

[77] Extinction of Customary Land Rights (Amendment) Order, 1969 (GN No. 260 of 1989).

international standards applicable to such restrictions. It also appears that the denial of movement and residence to the Barabaig on their traditional lands is unreasonable. First, their way of life is organized around pastoral activity and deep cultural connection with their ancestral lands. To deny them movement and residence on their traditional territory is to destroy their way of life and culture.[78]

Secondly, no alternative area has been offered for their resettlement, and even if such a social establishment were made available, it would not provide similar means of livelihood for the Barabaig in an economic, spiritual and cultural sense. Lack of consent on the part of Barabaig to resettle, absence of consultation and their having not participated in the process leading to their resettlement all point to the unreasonableness of the resettlement.

Thirdly, the restriction of movement and residence on the lands in question is not proportionate to the objective of agricultural development. As a pastoral group, the Barabaig are engaged in agricultural activity. The need for agricultural development in Tanzania generally cannot be isolated from the agricultural development of the Barabaig as a group, and their contribution in this respect to the country.

While the State may have a margin of appreciation in respect of restrictions on movement and residence within the State based upon public interest, its margin is considerably narrow because the grounds for restriction and the method thereof are defined. In other words, the State exercises a discretion fettered by the grounds on which restrictions on internal movement and residence may be permitted.

The relocation of the Barabaig is an example of the necessity for the protection of indigenous groups, particularly in view of desperate measures being taken by developing countries to try to develop their economies. The case adds further significance because of the fact that many developing countries in Africa and Asia deny the existence of indigenous groups within their territories.[79] Such denials must be irrelevant to the application of standards intended for the protection of indigenous people.

In fact it is not only indigenous groups that are affected by measures of resettlement in developing countries. Large sectors of ambient populations are increasingly being resettled to accommodate development projects because resettlement has become a development policy for attracting projects run by international development agencies. The fact that resettlement takes place at all points to the availability of land or territory for resettlement.

Usually the land acquired by forcing populations out of their traditional

[78] Africa Watch documents accounts of members of the Barabaig committing suicide by drowning in a sacred lake, and of their cattle dying because of the relocation.

[79] Some examples are India, Algeria, Tunisia, Malagasy.

places of habitat is rich, fertile, cleared, and has abundant resources. Rather than force indigenous groups and sectors of the general population out of such lands, the State must clear virgin land for projects initiated by it on behalf of or in conjunction with international agencies.

If the compensation paid to the resettled population is adequate in proportion to the value of the loss of property and land formerly occupied by it, then such compensation together with the cost of resettlement, should in theory be approximately equal to the cost of preparing virgin territory for development projects.

Hence, standards concerning relocation must be construed strictly and narrowly on defined grounds. These grounds should be limited to cases where the continued presence of the local population is endangered either by natural causes, or by necessary and important projects such as the construction of large-scale dams for hydro-electric power and large-scale irrigation.[80]

5. CONCLUSIONS

(1) Restrictions on the movement and residence of people which are intended for the protection of collective rights of indigenous groups to ownership of traditional lands and preservation of their traditional way of life are permissible in international law.

(2) Although the main human rights standards of general application are inadequate to deal with group rights, the principle of non-discrimination affords some protection in the context of equality of protection.

(3) The emerging standards for the protection of indigenous groups as contained in Convention 169 are to a certain extent evidenced by municipal standards relating to the protection of indigenous groups.

(4) There are major problems in the implementation of standards regarding the protection of group rights of indigenous people which involve an intricate balance of interests between individual rights and the rights of groups, and between indigenous groups and the ambient population. As these are problems of implementation, they will vary from State to State and no universal approach to the balancing of these interests can be laid.

[80] See Article 16 of Convention 169.

6

Restrictions on the Movement and Residence of Refugees

1. INTRODUCTION

This chapter discusses the legality, from the point of view of human rights, of restrictions placed on the movement and residence of refugees understood in the narrow classical international legal sense as persons seeking protection outside their country of origin.[1] There are two reasons for this choice of approach. Refugees have a distinct international legal status in respect of which specific standards applicable to their movement and residence in the host States exist under international treaties and other instruments for the protection of refugees.[2] Secondly, there is the need to harmonize these 'refugee specific' standards with those of human rights in addressing special problems concerning restrictions in the movement and residence of refugees to prisons, camps and settlements. Thus the distinction between the deprivation of liberty, and restriction of freedom of movement and residence which was discussed above in Chapter 3 should be recalled in this regard.

It is not intended to dwell on the problems surrounding the definition of refugees as such. As important as those problems are, they are not in issue for the present moment and, moreover, they have received authoritative treatment elsewhere.[3] Lest it be said, 'but definitional issues of minorities and indigenous groups have been dealt with at length, so why not those of refugees?', the simple answer is that unlike minorities and indigenous groups who normally reside within the territory of the country of origin, the definition of refugees has more to do with the criteria for establishing refugee status for the purpose of determining lawful entry and presence in the host country. The fact that there are standards related to restrictions on the movement and residence of refugees who are lawfully and unlawfully

[1] The phenomenon of the movement of persons displaced within States is omitted for the present moment because it overlaps significantly with other areas of law, such as the law of armed conflict, which are beyond the purview of the present work.

[2] See Articles 10, 26, and 31 of the Convention Relating to the Status of Refugees 1951, 189 U.N.T.S. 137, entry into force 1954; Article 1(6) of the Convention Governing Specific Aspects of Refugee Problems in Africa 1969, 14 U.N.T.S. 691, entry into force 1974; Article 9 of the Caracas Convention on Territorial Asylum 1954, OAS Official Records, OEA/Ser.X/1, entry into force 1954.

[3] Goodwin-Gill, *The Refugee in International Law*, 2nd edn. (Oxford, 1996).

present in host States renders a protracted discussion of the definition of refugees immaterial in the framework of the present study. However, as in the case of minorities, and as Goodwin-Gill[4] correctly points out, the term refugee is one of art, and it suffices to provide the reader with statements of the definitions contained in the international instruments for the protection of refugees.[5]

2. HUMAN RIGHTS AND RESTRICTIONS ON THE MOVEMENT OF REFUGEES

The problem of the freedom of movement and residence of refugees may be examined from three categories of restrictions, all of which are considered from the point of view of the pertinent human rights standards. Too often, the protection of refugees has suffered from the false dichotomy between 'refugee specific' standards, and human rights standards. The result is a reluctance on the part of many academics, practitioners, activists and States to apply human rights to asylum seekers and refugees.

This gap must be bridged in doctrine, as well as practice, in order to enhance the protection of refugees against the discretionary whims of States, at least where this discretion is in some ways fettered by defined international standards of behaviour as evidenced by the Convention Relating to the Status of Refugees 1951 as amended by the Protocol of 1967, and the Convention Governing Specific Aspects of the Refugee

[4] Goodwin-Gill, *The Refugee in International Law*, 2nd edn. (Oxford, 1996), at 3.

[5] Article 1(2) of the Convention Relating to the Status of Refugees, read together with Article 1(2) of the Protocol Relating to the Status of Refugees of 1967, define a refugee as any person who 'owing to a well-founded fear of being persecuted for reasons of race, religion, nationality, membership of a particular social group or political opinion and is outside the country of his nationality and is unable or owing to such fear, is unwilling to avail himself of the protection of that country; or who, not having a nationality and being outside the country of his former habitual residence . . . is unable or, owing to such fear is unwilling to return to it'. Under Article 1(2) of the Convention Governing Specific Aspects of Refugee Problems in Africa the term refugee also applies 'to every person who, owing to external aggression, occupation, foreign domination or events seriously disturbing internal order in either part or the whole of his country of origin or nationality, is compelled to leave the habitual place of residence in order to seek refuge in another place outside of the country of origin or nationality'. Under the Cartagena Declaration, adopted by Central American States meeting in Colombia in 1984, 'the definition or concept of refugee recommended for use in the region might, in addition to containing the elements from the 1951 Convention and the 1967 Protocol, also consider as refugees those persons that have fled from their countries because their life has been threatened by widespread violence, foreign aggression, domestic conflict, massive violation of human rights or other situations that have seriously disturbed public order'. See 'Colloquium on International Protection of Refugees in Central America, Mexico and Panama: Legal and Humanitarian Problems', Cartagena, Columbia, 19–22 November 1984. Reproduced in Norris, *Human Rights, The Inter-American System*, Part 5 (24. 11) (Oceana, 1986).

Problem in Africa 1969, and others. The application of the standards contained in those instruments must be seen in the light of subsequent developments in the field of human rights in international law.

The first category of restriction derives from the application of provisional measures to asylum seekers and refugees under Article 9 of the Convention Relating to the Status of Refugees.[6] Article 9 provides as follows:

> Nothing in this Convention shall prevent a Contracting State in time of war or other grave and exceptional circumstances, from taking provisional measures which it considers to be essential to the national security in the case of a particular person, pending a determination by the Contracting State that that person is in fact a refugee and that the continuance of such measures is necessary in his case in the interest of national security.

It is submitted that the use of provisional measures to restrict the movement and residence of asylum seekers and refugees is conditional upon the occurrence of war, or grave and exceptional circumstances. The principle of exceptional threat[7] applies here and the provisional measures envisaged by this provision are clearly in the form of the exercise of derogation which implies detention or deprivation of liberty. The standards on derogation, discussed below in Chapter 7, are applicable here.

There must be justification (proclamation and notice) for the existence of war, or grave or exceptional measures on grounds of national security; the measures must be taken pending the determination of refugee status (on a non-discriminatory basis); and the necessity on grounds of national security for the continued deprivation of liberty must be justified in relation to the detained refugee (proportionality), e.g., where a 'refugee' is a posing as a spy, or where he retains sensitive information regarding national security matters in his country of origin and has fled to seek protection so that it is both in his own, and in the national, interest to hold him or her securely.

In short, special powers attend to the application of this provision to special categories of asylum seekers and refugees. The experience of human rights standards shows that provisional measures offered in the language of Article 9 are not powers to be ordinarily exercised for the detention of ordinary refugees, a significant point missed by the guiding Conclusion of the Executive Committee (EXCOM) of the United Nations High Commissioner for Refugees on the matter of the detention of asylum seekers.[8] In the language of human rights, those powers must be exercised upon the existence of an exceptional threat to the security of the State and 'strictly to the exigencies of the situation'. Whether or not this is the case should be

[6] Goodwin-Gill, *The Refugee*, n. 3 above, ch. 7.

[7] See further below Chapter 7, pp. 132–5.

[8] Conclusion No. 44 (XXXVII), 1986.

subject to international legal scrutiny of the provisional measures taken, bearing in mind that the State is obliged to provide appropriate justification for detaining persons.

The second category of restrictions applies to the situation of the unlawful entry of asylum seekers under Article 31 of the Convention Relating to the Status of Refugees. The requirement for 'unlawful entry' for persons fleeing from obvious risks is a misnomer; entry by itself is crucially not prohibited on the part of asylum seekers, although experience shows otherwise. The movement and residence of asylum seekers or refugees who make a direct illegal entry from a territory where their life or freedom was threatened, owing to a well-founded fear of persecution, may be restricted. But that provision prohibits States from applying restrictions, other than those which are necessary, and such restrictions shall only be applied until the status of asylum seekers in the country is regularized, or they obtain admission into another country.

In human rights terms, the use of 'restrictions' under Article 31 does not imply detention, although this may have been the intention, and the difference between detention and restriction (see Chapter 3) must be upheld as a matter of principle and degree. The placement of asylum seekers in prisons constitutes a deprivation of liberty, but the requirement for asylum seekers to reside in a specified area, or not to move out of designated areas without prior authorization, or detention for a short period, amounts to a restriction of movement. The purpose or legality of restrictions under Article 31 is to enable the process of determining the identity and status of the claimant, and the restrictions should clearly be temporary, and conditional upon formal recognition of refugee status, or departure to a foreign country. In the case of *A v Australia*,[9] where an asylum seeker was held for a period of four years, the Human Rights Committee took the view that 'the fact of illegal entry may indicate a need for investigation and there may be other factors particular to the individual, such as the likelihood of absconding and lack of cooperation, which may justify detention for a period. Without such factors detention may be considered arbitrary, even if entry was illegal'.

On the merits of the question in issue, the Committee concluded that the detention of the applicant for a period of over four years was arbitrary within the meaning of Article 9(1) of the Covenant on Civil and Political Rights and that the State had failed to advance any grounds which justified continued detention for over four years.

The prohibition on restrictions 'other than those that are necessary' has a clear echo in general human rights standards and the content of that phrase must be verified by reference to the public interest grounds on which restrictions are necessary and to which Chapter 2 refers. A special problem

[9] Communication No. 560/1993, CCPR/C/59/D/560/1993, at 23–4.

connected with the use of such restrictions concerns the mass influx of refugees and the application of Article 31 of the Convention Relating to the Status of Refugees.[10] The Executive Committee of the United High Commissioner for Refugees[11] has laid down certain guiding principles for the conduct of States during large-scale influxes of refugees or asylum seekers under Article 31 which are consistent with principles of human rights. As a minimum standard, refugees arriving *en masse* should not be subjected to restrictions on their movements, other than those which are necessary in the interest of public health and public order. However, public security as a ground for restricting the movement of asylum seekers and refugees has assumed added significance in the light of refugee flows from internal armed conflicts which are mixed with armed military personnel and it seems acceptable to isolate or separate out the latter by means of restricted movement from the ordinary civilian refugees and the host population.

The final category comprises the ordinary application of restrictions to refugees with status, that is, those lawfully in the host country by virtue of a positive determination of their official status as refugees in the host State. Standards concerning the movement and residence of such refugees are expressed in Article 26 of the Convention Relating to the Status of Refugees:

> Each Contracting State shall accord to refugees lawfully in its territory the right to choose their place of residence and to move freely within its territory, subject to any regulations applicable to aliens generally in the same circumstances.

The Convention applies to this category of refugees an international minimum standard of treatment applicable in the same circumstances to aliens with regard to freedom of movement and residence. The phrase 'in the same circumstances' is described in Article 6 of the Convention as implying any requirements including those concerning length and conditions of sojourn or residence which particular individual refugees would have to fulfil for the enjoyment of the right in question. In this case, the requirement of lawful presence in State territory as a result of the determination of refugee status should be taken as a condition for free movement and choice of residence. Equally, those seeking asylum who have entered the territory of the host State by lawful means prior to the determination of their refugee claim may have the benefit of freedom of movement and residence as aliens or in the same circumstances as aliens. The provisions of Article 26 raise the issue of human rights and the international minimum standard of treatment in the context of whether refugees should

[10] A similar view is expressed in Goodwin-Gill, *The Refugee*, n. 3 above, 247.

[11] Executive Committee of the United Nations High Commissioner for Refugees, *Conclusions on the International Protection of Refugees, No. 22 (XXXII) Protection of Asylum-Seekers in Situations of Large Scale Influx* (Geneva, 1990), 50.

be treated according to the former or the latter. The strength behind the international minimum standard has always been in the protective role played by the State of origin in the diplomatic protection of its nationals abroad. Because refugees lack the protection of their State of origin, the potential strength of the principle is lost on that basis. But that is not the only sense in which that standard applies. Its advantage is that States have traditionally been more familiar with it than the emergent human rights standards and this certainly was the case in 1951 when the Convention was adopted.

The two standards co-exist and should benefit refugees mutually. The international minimum standard benefits refugees in the sense of the quality of residency which they enjoy in the practice of many Western States, i.e. their status as refugees entitles them to acquire official residential status after a certain period in the same circumstances as aliens. Consequently, the subsequent cessation of refugees' status offers them a choice to remain as ordinary immigrants with official leave to remain, or to return to their countries of origin. Much of this appears to be in the realm of the discretion of the host States but in substance the practice is based on the international minimum standard of treatment for aliens or foreign nationals.

Progress in the field of human rights is such that there is a stronger means of protecting the right of refugees to free movement and choice of residence even if this can be restricted to designated places. The Human Rights Committee[12] has taken the position that, in relation to aliens, consent for entry may be given subject to conditions relating, for example, to movement, residence and employment. However:

> Once an alien is lawfully within a territory [of a state], his (her) freedom of movement within the territory and his (her) right to leave that territory may only be restricted in accordance with Article 12, paragraph 3 [of the Covenant on Civil and Political Rights]. Differences in treatment in this regard between aliens and nationals, or between different categories of aliens, need to be justified under Article 12, paragraph 3.

This statement applies fully to refugees, and the Committee is not alone in expressing this view. Harris[13] comments helpfully when he observes that:

> to the extent that customary international law imposes human rights obligations upon States, it may be that the standards set by those obligations will be seen as identical to those required by the international minimum standard and, since they bind States in the treatment of their own nationals, as a part of a national treatment requirement too.

[12] *General Comments* CCPR/C/21/Rev.1/Add.1, at 17.

[13] Harris, *Cases and Materials, on International Law*, 4th edn. (London, 1995), 499, 520.

Nevertheless, it remains a controversial question in international law as to whether an alien is entitled to the protection of an international minimum standard of treatment or only to equality of treatment with the nationals of the State concerned, i.e., national treatment.

A brief survey of the position taken by States, as evidenced by some of the reservations entered to Article 26 of the Convention Relating to the Status of Refugees, shows a recognition, in some respects, of human rights-based standards applicable to restrictions on internal movement and residence,[14] particularly in regard to the public interest grounds on which movement and residence may be restricted.

Angola has reserved the right to prescribe, transfer or circumscribe the place of residence of certain refugees or groups of refugees, and to restrict their freedom of movement, whenever considerations of national or international order make it advisable to do so. Such considerations of national or international order are likely to include restrictions on the movement and residence of refugees on account of public order or *ordre public*, national security, and international law security.

In its reservation, Greece has declared that in cases or circumstances which, in its opinion would justify exceptional procedure for reasons of national security or public order, it reserves the right to derogate from the provisions of Article 26. This reservation is inappropriate because it relates to derogation rather than ordinary restriction, and it should have been more appropriately made by reference to Article 9 of the Convention.

Mozambique has stated that it reserves the right to designate a place or places of principal residence for refugees or to restrict their movement and residence in the interest of national security. The Netherlands has also reserved the right to designate a place of principal residence for certain refugees or groups of refugees in the public interest. Rwanda cited reasons of public policy (*ordre public*) as a ground for reserving the right to determine the place of residence of refugees, and to establish limits to their freedom of movement.

Zambia and Zimbabwe have entered similarly worded reservations to Article 26, preserving their right to designate a place or places of residence for refugees. The reservations do not stipulate the grounds for doing so, although the relevant pieces of domestic legislation allude to the maintenance of public order.[15] Opinions of writers help to elucidate applicable standards on restrictions relating to the right of refugees to move and reside within States. One view is that Article 26 would not be breached in

[14] See United Nations, *Status of International Instruments* (New York, 1987). Botswana, Sudan, Iran, Guatemala, Papua New Guinea, and Spain have entered reservations of a general nature concerning or affecting the movement and residence of refugees in their territories. See also Goodwin-Gill, *The Refugee in International Law* (Oxford, 1983), 153.

[15] Zambia Refugee (Control) Act 1970, s. 12; Zimbabwe Refugee Act 1983, s. 12.

the case of special situations where refugees have to be accommodated in special camps or in special areas, even if this does not apply to aliens generally.[16]

The question of restricting the movement and residence of refugees to camps or scheme settlements is discussed below in connection with regional standards. For the moment, it suffices to note briefly, that it is of importance to the rights of refugees generally, that they should not be held in conditions similar to those of prisoners, or persons suffering internal banishment by virtue of restrictions which confine their movement and residence to camps or scheme settlements.

Another view is that Article 26 would not be infringed where, under a contract of labour, or group resettlement scheme, refugees were required to remain in a particular job in a certain area for a particular time. This view was prevalent during the preparation of the Convention Relating to the Status of Refugees.[17] Problems connected with restrictions in this context have been elaborated by Prince Aga Khan,[18] a former United Nations High Commissioner for Refugees.

The Prince noted that although the principle of the free choice of place of residence is very widely accepted, its application is sometimes hampered by the regulations on access to employment. He observes that, in fact, a work permit granted to refugees, especially new arrivals, frequently turns out to be valid only for a specific administrative district:

> The situation is worse in some African countries, in particular, where large groups of refugees have been settled in regions carefully chosen for collective rural settlement. In those cases—in Tanzania and the Sudan, for example—there is sometimes a tendency to regard permission to stay as linked to the place of settlement where refugees are assured of being able to work and thus support themselves, which would not be the case in just any part of the country, particularly in the towns.[19]

Some observations may be made with respect to such controls. Although residence may be tied to a specific area of employment, the principle of choice of residence within such an area is applicable. Refugees, as well as other persons, who reside within the said area by virtue of employment may be free to move within and out of the area to other places in the country subject only to limitations which are acceptable in accordance with international standards relating to the right of movement and residence within States. In addition, care should be taken to ensure that the requirement to reside within the area in which refugees or other persons are employed does not amount to forced or compulsory labour. Such requirements are sometimes part of a regime of economic planning or development where the margin between the planned use of labour and the direction of labour, or

[16] Goodwin-Gill, *The Refugee*, n. 3 above, p. 251.
[17] UN doc. E/AC.32/SR.11, 6.
[18] Khan, 'Refugees and Displaced Persons', (1976)I *Recueil* 324.
[19] Ibid.

between free and compulsory mobilization of labour for purposes of economic development, is both narrow and delicate.[20]

Most of these requirements may admittedly affect the movement and residence of categories of other persons within the State. But refugees are obviously more vulnerable to restrictions which may directly or indirectly effect a system of forced or compulsory labour. It is hence useful to consider very briefly the application of this term in situations where the right of movement and residence is restricted to certain locations or areas of employment.

The term 'forced or compulsory labour' has been noted to be one of art, at least in legal usage.[21] According to ILO Convention 29, which came into force in 1932, forced or compulsory labour is defined to mean all work, or service which is exacted from any person under the menace of a penalty, and for which the said person has not offered voluntarily.

Convention 105, concluded in 1957 by ILO, and entered into force in 1959, amplifies upon the content of forced or compulsory labour. It prohibits, and prescribes for the suppression of, any form of forced or compulsory labour used:

(a) as a means of political coercion or education, or as a punishment for holding, or expressing political views or views ideologically opposed to the established political, social, or economic system;
(b) as a method of mobilizing and using labour for purposes of economic development;
(c) as a means of labour discipline;
(d) as a punishment for having participated in strikes; and
(e) as a means of racial, social, national or religious discrimination.

In the *Iversen*[22] case, the European Commission for Human Rights considered the question of forced labour in relation to Article 4(2) of the European Convention on Human Rights and Fundamental Freedoms. This provision states that no one shall be required to perform forced or compulsory labour.[23] The applicant, Iversen, was a qualified dentist and applied

[20] Fawcett, *The Application of the European Convention on Human Rights*, 2nd edn. (Oxford 1987), 58.

[21] Ibid. 56.

[22] 1468/62:6 *Yearbook* 278–332; Fawcett, *Application*, n. 20 above, 58–61.

[23] From this stipulation Article 4(3) excludes; (a) any work required to be done in the ordinary course of detention imposed according to the provisions of Article 5 of the Convention or during conditional release from such detention; (b) any service of a military character or, in case of conscientious objectors in countries where they are recognized, service exacted instead of compulsory military service; (c) any service exacted in case of an emergency or calamity threatening the life or well-being of the community; (d) any work or service which forms part of normal civic obligations. Fawcett comments that while (a) and (b) are true exceptions to the prohibition of forced labour, it is possible to read (c) and (d) as belonging to a different order. His view is that what is accepted as a natural duty to the community may or should be so recognized by the individual, and work or service under (c) and (d) may be done willingly as a duty; work or service recognized as such by the individual does not amount to forced or compulsory labour at all and does not constitute exceptions to the prohibition of forced or compulsory labour. See Fawcett, *Application* n. 20 above, 58.

for a post in the public dental service in Southern Norway. The application was rejected and the applicant was directed under the Provisional Act 1956 to take a position in the service in the Moskenes district in Northern Norway for one year. Following a protest, the applicant accepted the post in January 1960 and left it in May 1960, having indicated his intention to leave earlier in March. In the wake of proceedings which were brought against him under the said Act, the applicant was ordered to pay a certain fine or go to prison for 30 days. His application to the Norwegian Supreme Court on grounds that the Provisional Act was contrary to both the constitution and Article 4 of the Convention was dismissed.[24]

The Commission found that the expression 'forced or compulsory labour' was not defined in the law and no authoritative description of what it comprises was to be found elsewhere. It observed that the concept of compulsory or forced labour could not be understood solely in terms of the literal meaning of the words, and had in fact come to be regarded, in international law and practice, as evidenced in part by the provisions and applications of the ILO Convention and Resolutions on Forced Labour, as having certain elements.

It was therefore reasonable, in the interpretation of Article 4(2) of the Convention, to have due regard to those elements: first, that the work or service is performed by the worker against his or her will; and secondly, the requirement that the work or service to be performed is unjust or oppressive or the work or service itself involves avoidable hardship. On the facts of the case, the Commission conceded that the Provisional Act imposed obligatory service. However, the Commission took note of the following: that the service was for a short duration and provided favourable remuneration; it did not involve any diversion from chosen professional work and was only applied in the case of posts not filled after being duly advertised; no discriminatory, arbitrary or punitive application was involved; and the requirement to perform the service was not unjust or oppressive.

Accordingly, the Commission held that the Provisional Act was properly applied to Iversen when he was directed to take up the post at Moskenes. A dissenting minority opinion expressed a contrary view. It gave weight to the fact that conditions under which the applicant was required to perform his work in Moskenes as regards salary, time limit and professional facilities did not as such exclude the applicability of Article 4(2) of the

[24] The Supreme Court of Norway held that the protection against forced or compulsory labour was not reasonably applicable to obligations of a public nature in Iversen's case. The court was of the view that the work in question was of a short duration, well paid, based on the professional qualifications of the person concerned, and was in immediate continuation of his completed studies.

Convention because the work in question was imposed upon the applicant subject to penal sanction.

The relevance of the *Iversen* case in relation to restrictions on internal movement and residence generally is that the conditions of employment of the applicant required him to reside in a particular district of the country. Where conditions of employment generally, including those of refugees, restrict movement and residence to certain areas, and enforce forced or compulsory labour because that work or service is performed against one's will subject to penal sanction, and is unjust, or oppressive, or involves avoidable hardship, the restrictions on movement and residence in that context would be unjustified on grounds of reasonableness, and also on the requirement that restrictions ought to be consistent with the enjoyment of other rights.

3. REFUGEES AND FREEDOM OF MOVEMENT UNDER REGIONAL REGIMES

Specific standards on the movement and residence of refugees have emerged in the context of the efforts made by regional bodies to tackle the issue of refugees on a regional basis. In so far as the requirements of relevance permit, the standards examined under this heading are those contained in the regional instruments formulated by the Organization of African Unity in Africa, the Organization of American States in South America, and the European Union in Europe, relating to refugees lawfully present in Africa, South America, and Europe.

(i) Restrictions under the O.A.U. Convention

The Convention Governing the Specific Aspects of Refugee Problems 1969 in Africa obliges Member States of the O.A.U. to use their best endeavours consistent with their respective legislation 'to receive and to secure the settlement of refugees within their territories'. In consequence, many African States have adopted the practice of establishing scheme settlements or camps as a mode of settling refugees in situations of mass influx. The Convention itself makes no specific provision regarding the method of settlement of refugees, but lays certain requirements which affect the settlement of refugees and constrain their movement and residence in the receiving States.

These requirements relate to the principle of safe location of refugees, and the prohibition against subversive activities. With respect to safe location, the Convention stipulates that for reasons of security, countries of asylum shall, as far as possible, settle refugees at a reasonable distance from the frontier of their country of origin.[25] The principle of safe location of

[25] Article II(6).

refugees originated from Latin American practice where it was developed for the physical protection of refugees against hostile acts directed against them from their countries of origin.[26]

By contrast, the prohibition against subversive activities is intended to promote harmonious relations between African States. Hence Article III of the Convention states that all refugees have duties to the country in which they find themselves. They are required in particular to conform to the laws and regulations of the receiving State as well as measures taken for the maintenance of public order within those States.

This provision expressly obliges refugees to abstain from any subversive activities against any Member State of the O.A.U. It further obliges State parties to prohibit refugees residing in their territories from attacking any Member State of the O.A.U. by any activity which is likely to cause tension between Member States, and in particular by use of arms, through the press, or by radio. The prohibition against subversive activities on the part of refugees is a vital condition for the entitlement of refugees to protection in Africa. However, the term 'subversive activities' is itself wide and vague; indication of its meaning can be glimpsed from the way in which it is used in other instruments adopted by the O.A.U. Foremost of these is the Charter of the Organization of African Unity 1963 which sets out to achieve unity, co-operation and solidarity between African States. To this end, the Charter unreservedly condemns political assassination, as well as subversive activities on the part of neighbouring States, or any other State.[27] Furthermore, the O.A.U.'s Declaration on the Problem of Subversion of 1965 calls for intolerance against any subversion originating only in African countries against another Member State of the O.A.U. Although the Declaration is not binding, it provides evidence of the position and attitudes of African States on the question of subversion.

It would appear that the rationale behind the prohibition on subversive activities is to express political solidarity between African countries and the prohibition is a safeguard against possible external interference in what were then seen as internal affairs. Thus the Declaration undertakes 'to oppose collectively and firmly by every means at our disposal every form of subversion conceived, organised or financed by foreign powers against Africa, the O.A.U. or its Member States individually'.

The prohibition against refugee involvement in subversive activities and the necessity for them to be safely located for reasons of security, and the

[26] There are instances in which refugees have been killed in the country of asylum by agents of the country of origin, or physically abducted from the territory of the country of asylum to the country of origin in Africa. See for example, *News From Africa Watch*, 24 April 1989, 26 October 1989.

[27] Articles II and III(5).

desire to prevent refugees from arriving in urban areas may seem to account for restrictions placed on their movement and residence in camps or scheme settlements in Africa. In reality many African States restrict the movement of refugees to settlements close to the frontier with the country of origin with the consequence that cross-border movements, including the smuggling of arms, are inevitable.

In principle, however, restrictions which may be applied generally to limit the movement and residence of refugees as a matter of safe location are permissible. The purpose of such restrictions must be to ensure the safety of refugees as well as the civilian and humanitarian character of the refugee system. Nonetheless, the restrictions must be proportionate to these objectives in the sense that their application should be limited to specific areas, particularly those which are close to the border with stricken countries of origin, where the safety of refugees and the security of the host State are likely to be endangered.

The Executive Committee[28] has expressed the view that the location of asylum-seekers should be determined by their safety and well-being, as well as by the security needs of the receiving State. It recommends that asylum seekers should, as far as possible, be located at a reasonable distance from the frontier of their country of origin, and that refugees should not become involved in subversive activities against their country of origin or any other State. The breach of this principle accounted, in part, for the deaths of many Rwandese refugees in Eastern Zaire (Democratic Republic of the Congo) in 1996 and 1997. Given that the prohibition on subversive activities also affirms the character of refugee protection as a peaceful humanitarian act in fostering friendly relations between States, it was with little surprise that the disregard of these principles in 1998 led to internal civil strife and external military intervention in the Democratic Republic of the Congo by States (Rwanda and Uganda) whose geo-political security is threatened by armed incursions from refugee camps in the Congo. The Congo, in turn, obtained military help from Zimbabwe, Namibia, and Angola, thus raising the prospect for a wider regional conflict. The lesson to be drawn is that humanitarian principles and obligations underlying refugee protection have a certain logic which reinforces the system of international order, particularly the customary prohibition on the use of force against the political independence and territorial integrity of States.[29]

Therefore restrictions which are placed to limit the movement and residence of refugees on the ground of prohibiting objective subversive

[28] Executive Committee of the United Nations High Commissioner for Refugees, *Conclusions on the International Protection of Refugees*, 50.

[29] Brownlie, *International Law and the Use of Force By States* (Oxford, 1963), 112–29, 361–8; *Nicaragua v United States* (1986) I.C.J. Rep. 1.

activities against States of origin or other interested States play a role in maintaining the international protection of refugees as a peaceful and humanitarian act. However, the use of restrictions can be questionable in other contexts. Cynics may point out, with some justification, that such restrictions are part of the policy of containment which views refugees as a possible source of subversion against their countries of origin even when the grounds for 'subversion' are objectively justifiable, as in the case of the removal of Milton Obote from his second tenure as President of Uganda in 1986 by the National Resistance Movement whose support base included refugees. The Declaration on the Problem of Subversion reflects this dilemma. In one part, the Declaration envisages the strict observance of the principles of international law applicable to political refugees. In another part, it calls for the guarantee of the safety of political refugees and support for them in the struggle to liberate their countries, while curiously omitting political refugees from independent African States.[30]

The assumption is that the safety of such refugees cannot be guaranteed, nor can they enjoy the right of self-determination and certain rights which are prohibited as incidents of subversive activities. Such rights include freedom of speech and freedom of expression in relation to use of the press and radio against, say, oppressive policies in their countries of origin.[31]

Restrictions regarding the movement and residence of refugees within States in connection with the prevention of subversive activities may only be permitted with respect to particular individual refugees. Commenting on the Latin American treaties which uphold the principle of safe location as a means of preventing subversive activities against their countries of origin, Madsen made the appropriate observation that this regime may only be implemented in cases where there exists a real concern that the refugees in question may engage in subversive activities. Madsen also expressed the opinion that if no such concern is justified, the application of measures of safe location would probably conflict with Article 26 of the Convention Relating to the Status of Refugees.[32] To justify restriction of movement and residence of refugees in the context of preventing subversive activities, there must be clear evidence of involvement in subversion and moreover, such measures may be unjustified where the prevention of so-called subversive activities conflicts with a legitimate exercise of the right to self-determination.

However, apart from considerations relating to safe location and the prevention of subversive activities, there is an underlying factor concerning the

[30] See Article 8 of the Declaration.

[31] In 1989 Africa Watch noted with deep concern that evidence showing that the rights of refugees who were considered in Djibouti to be antagonistic to neighbouring regimes were systematically and sharply curtailed in the political interest.

[32] Madsen, 'Political Rights and Freedoms of Refugees', in Melander and Nobel (eds), *African Refugees and the Law* (Uppsala, 1978), 48.

erection of camps and settlements for refugees in Africa and elsewhere. The massive influx of refugees into receiving countries requires a system of order for dealing with refugees on arrival, although this does not necessarily justify the regime of camps at all times. Arguably, a sudden influx of a large number of refugees in State territory outside the normal process of immigration is a public order matter and restrictions which are applied in the context of designating places of residence in these circumstances have a legitimate objective. For example, a group or groups of refugees may need protection against a hostile local population, or section of the refugee population. In this respect, restrictions may serve not only the purpose of establishing designated places of residence for refugees, but also that of protecting them by limiting general movement and residence to such zones or areas within which their liberty of movement can be exercised. Each case has to be assessed on its own merits.

The establishment of regional economic and political communities in Africa will impact upon the movement and residence of refugees within these entities, particularly in ECOWAS in West Africa, SADC in Southern Africa, and IGAD in East Africa. The emerging regimes on free movement in these regions reaffirm commitment to the obligations for the protection of refugees under the Convention Relating to the Status of Refugees and the African Convention Governing the Specific Aspects of the Refugee Problem in Africa. Consequently the preceding analysis in respect of the freedom of movement and residence of refugees applies to these entities.

However, the specific mode of application of the standards and the pattern of movement will vary according to the structures of refugee management and policy within the overall objectives of the framework for free movement in general. Within ECOWAS, refugees in theory are entitled to free movement throughout that region, but in practice their freedom of movement and residence is constrained by the system of managing refugee movements. Identity cards and the system of food distribution ties refugees to specific countries and places within those countries, e.g., Ivory Coast and Senegal, with the consequence that refugees cannot receive assistance outside those areas and countries. Refugees from Liberia may receive protection in Ivory Coast if they reside within designated zones; they may be permitted to move outside the designated *zone d'accueil* on the authority of a temporary travel permit if they can establish a temporary necessity for such movement. Refugees from Sierra-Leone may not receive assistance or recognition in Senegal because Senegal is not designated as a country of protection for them.[33]

In SADC and IGAD more emphasis is placed on fostering durable solutions common to the root causes of the problem of refugees and other

[33] Lawyers' Committee for Human Rights, *African Exodus* (New York, 1995), 47–104.

involuntary population movements in those regions, based on interdisciplinary approaches to the humanitarian, economic, social, human rights and environmental aspects of refugee situations.[34] The measures canvassed to achieve this end aim at establishing a co-ordinating mechanism for early warning of refugee movements and the resolution of conflicts likely to produce refugees; enhancing the capacity of Member States to implement internationally accepted principles and standards for the protection of refugees; building awareness within the general public and the media on human rights and the plight of asylum seekers and refugees; the harmonization of policies, legislation, procedures and assistance pertaining to refugees; maintenance of a database containing information on refugee movements, with the sole aim of determining which of the Member States is responsible for assessing an asylum claim. The problem of harmonization must be examined at two levels: first, the harmonization of the regional free movement regime with that of international obligations for the protection of refugees, including those on freedom of movement which have been discussed above; secondly, the harmonization of domestic legislation between the Member States in such a way that it reflects or incorporates the harmonized regime of free movement in general, and the movement and residence of refugees and asylum seekers specifically.

The question of determining which Member State is responsible for assessing an asylum claim appears at first to be a relic of the recent developments in the European Union. In substance, this practice has existed informally in Africa with respect to individual urban asylum seekers and refugees. In ECOWAS the same practice has been applied to situations of mass influxes on an informal basis and, as noted, the effect there is to restrict the entry and movement of refugees from specific countries to certain receiving countries.

There is merit, in the context of free movement regimes, in the idea that States should not avoid exercising their responsibility to determine claims for refugee protection in order to curtail indeterminate irregular movements in which asylum seekers are 'ping-balled' from one State to another. Two considerations are called for in establishing a dual system of State responsibility for determining refugee protection on one hand, and the avoidance of 'ping-balling' refugees from State to State on the other hand. One is that the standards and procedures for dealing with refugee claims should be uniform so that refugees are not prejudiced by the oddity of the particular State dealing with their claim. The two-stage harmonization process suggested above has pointed relevance here. In the second place, the standards of the African Convention which relate to the practice of

[34] See Chapter XII, Articles 45–50 of the Protocol on the Free Movement of Persons in the Southern African Development Community.

'group eligibility' to refugee protection should be taken to be predominant in setting the method or procedure for entertaining claims for refugee protection given the specific character of massive refugee flows in Africa.

(ii) The movement of refugees and the Caracas Convention

Standards concerning the treatment of refugees in South America have developed over a fairly long period of time.[35] However, the standards which are applicable to restrictions on the movement and residence of refugees appear in the Caracas Convention on Territorial Asylum 1954. As in the case of Africa, these standards relate to the safe location of refugees from their countries of origin in order to prevent subversive activities. But the element of 'subversive' and the process for dealing with it is better handled than in the African Convention. In this regard, Article 8 of the Caracas Convention on Territorial Asylum provides as follows:

> At the request of the interested State, the State that has granted refuge or asylum shall take steps to keep watch over, or to intern at a reasonable distance from its border, those political refugees or asylees who are notorious leaders of a subversive movement, as well as those against whom there is evidence that they are disposed to join it. Determination of the reasonable distance from the border, for the purpose of internment, shall depend upon the judgment of the authorities of the state of refuge. All expenses incurred as a result of the internment of political asylees and refugees shall be chargeable to the state that makes the request.

Standards concerning restrictions on the movement and residence of refugees in the South American States appear to be limited in application to the situation of political refugees who are notorious leaders of subversive movements or those likely to join such movements. They may also only be applied at the instance of the requesting State to situate such refugees at a safe distance from the borders of countries of origin. In terms of legality, the proportionality of restrictions on movement is clearly measurable by the element of the presence of politically subversive refugees while the process of restriction should be circumscribed by request. In practice, the sheer pressure resulting from the heavy responsibility of hosting large numbers of refugees in South America has led to the establishment of camps or scheme settlements for refugees within which movement and residence is restricted. In its report on *Displaced Persons in the Region and Protection of Refugees*, the Inter-American Commission lamented that the existing standards under various instruments on refugees in South America were inadequate to deal with current conditions of the flow of displaced persons.

[35] Havana Convention on Asylum 1928; Montevideo Convention on Political Asylum 1933; Caracas Convention on Territorial Asylum 1954; Caracas Convention on Diplomatic Asylum 1954.

One of the reasons advanced by the Commission for this state of affairs was that political asylum in South America presently involved large masses of people; previously, it was granted only in cases of persecution against well-known political leaders or a very small group of people. This development has created the problem of the resettlement of refugees in camps or settlements which has given rise to human rights concerns. Perhaps for this reason, and for its commitment to human rights, the Commission wholly approved the text of the conclusions of the Declaration of Cartagena 1984 as a basis for solving problems of refugee protection in South America. The Declaration endorsed the safe location of refugee camps and settlements away from border areas, stating that they should be established at a reasonable distance from the borders of the host States. It further called for the improvement of the conditions of protection for refugees, the preservation of their human rights, implementation of projects aimed at their self-sufficiency, and their integration into the society of the receiving State. The refreshing thing about the Declaration of Cartagena is the manner in which the problem of settlements and camps is addressed in the context of freedom of movement and residence, and of refugee protection as being inclusive of human rights protection.

4. THE FREE MOVEMENT OF REFUGEES IN THE EUROPEAN UNION AND THE TREATY OF AMSTERDAM

Correlative to the establishment of an internal area of free movement in the European Union is the erection of strict external border controls in the field of immigration and with specific respect to the entry of asylum seekers. The Treaty of Amsterdam envisages the adoption of strict immigration and asylum controls in accordance with the Convention and Protocol Relating to the Status of Refugees and other relevant treaties, within five years of the entry of that treaty into force. In reality such measures exist already under an array of certain treaties in force in the European Union which the Treaty of Amsterdam codifies. Mention has been made of these treaties previously in Chapter 3 and only relevant references to them will be made here in appropriate contexts.

Article 63 of the Treaty of Amsterdam (Article 73k in the Maastricht Treaty) lists the measures for adoption by the Council of Europe within the following areas.

(a) *Criteria and mechanisms for determining which Member State is responsible for considering an application for asylum submitted by a third country national in one of the Member States*. It is to be noted that this measure is now in force under the terms of what is commonly known as the Dublin Convention, i.e. Convention Determining the State Responsible for

Examining Applications for Asylum Lodged in One of the Member States of the Community 1990.[36] The benefits and constraints of this measure have been noted above but the ever growing potential for restrictionist tendencies in attempting to control the inflow of asylum seekers cannot be discounted.

(b) *Minimum standards on the reception of asylum seekers in Member States.* These standards invariably include the necessity for asylum seekers to be in possession of valid entry visas and the imposition of financial liability on the part of public air carrier lines,[37] the detention and, or, restriction of the movement of asylum seekers on arrival in designated centres pursuant to a policy of 'humane deterrence' and curtailment of the quality of social welfare given to asylum seekers.

Some of these measures have hitherto been deplored by the Council of Europe,[38] and the preceding analysis of Article 31 of the Convention Relating to the Status of Refugees shows that the detention of asylum seekers would appear to be unlawful by the terms of that provision as well as by reference to human rights standards. To this effect, the decision of the Human Rights Committee in *A v Australia* is illustrative and it is reinforced by the decision of the European Commission in the case of *Amuur v France*[39] where the holding of an asylum seeker at an airport in France was held to be a breach of the right to personal liberty under Article 5 of the European Convention on Human Rights.

For the States parties, and in so far as the measures targeted by the Amsterdam Treaty pay homage to the Convention Relating to the Status of Refugees, there is a duty on the part of public authorities to provide refugees with accommodation in the same circumstances as aliens under Article 22 of that Convention, and Article 23 obliges the Contracting States to accord refugees lawfully staying in their countries public relief and assistance as is accorded to their nationals. These obligations would appear to extend to asylum seekers lawfully present or in relation to whom it would be unlawful to return to their countries of origin on account of the prohibition on refoulement, i.e. returning or expelling asylum seekers to States where their lives or freedoms are at risk (Article 33), or the prohibition on torture, inhuman and degrading treatment (Article 3 of the European Convention on Human Rights).[40] Thus in *R v Hammersmith and Fulham LBC, ex parte M* the High Court invoked a duty of care and attention upon

[36] For text, see European Document CONV/ASILE.

[37] See Council of Europe Recommendation 1163 (1991) on the Arrival of Asylum Seekers at European Airports, adopted by the Parliamentary Assembly of the Council of Europe on 23 September 1991.

[38] Ibid.; Council of Europe Order 447 (1991).

[39] European Commission Decision 22 (1996).

[40] *Chahal v United Kingdom*, (1996) 23 EHRR 278; *Ahmed v Austria*, (1996) 24 EHRR 278.

a local authority in terms of the National Assistance Act 1948 with regard to an asylum seeker who had no money and who lacked the means to support himself.[41] In addition, the Parliamentary Assembly of the Council of Europe has invited Member States to provide sufficient accommodation and acceptable humanitarian treatment for asylum seekers awaiting the first decision on their request for asylum.

(c) *Minimum standards with respect to the qualification of third-country nationals as refugees.* The quest for appropriate standards is evident when it is considered that the current stock of existing measures includes the classification of certain countries as safe countries from which no claims for asylum can be entertained, the need for direct entry or movement from the country of origin as a pre-condition for admission, and that asylum seekers may be re-routed to third safe countries of asylum. Devices of this sort may be regarded as amounting to the avoidance of international obligations to provide protection to refugees.[42] Protocol 6 to the Amsterdam Treaty practically precludes asylum seekers from amongst the nationals of the Member States of the European Union on grounds that these States are regarded as safe countries of origin and any applications emanating from their nationals are presumed to be manifestly unfounded. This ignores the problem of the Roma or Gypsies.

(d) *Minimum standards on procedures in Member States for granting or withdrawing refugee status.* The major factor is the harmonization[43] of status determination procedures as a result of the obligations pertaining to the single State system for responsibility for determining refugee status which emanate from the Dublin Convention. However, the measures in existence include manifestly unfounded claims for refugee protection,[44] accelerated and limited appellate systems, and the rapid removal of unsuccessful claimants. These measures interact with those discussed in (c) above.

Finally, the Treaty of Amsterdam places the *ad hoc* system of temporary protection[45] which emerged in Europe in response to the plight of large numbers of Bosnian refugees in the early 1990s on a treaty base. Minimum standards for temporary protection are targeted for prescription in order to provide a legal basis for extending temporary protection, by definition, to displaced persons from third countries who cannot return to their

[41] *The Times*, 10 October 1996; *R v Secretary of State for Social Security, ex parte Joint Council for the Welfare of Immigrants, The Times*, 27 June 1996.

[42] *R v Special Adjudicator, ex parte Turus, The Times*, 13 May 1996; Leigh and Beyani, *Blackstone's Guide to the Asylum and Immigration Act 1996* (London, 1996), 11–12.

[43] Resolution A3-0337/92 on the Harmonization within the European Community of Asylum Law and Policies 1992.

[44] *R v Secretary of State, ex parte Mehari and Others* [1994] Q.B. 474; *R v Secretary of State for the Home Department, ex parte Abdi and Gawe* [1996] 1 W.L.R. 298.

[45] For the appropriate usage of this concept see Goodwin-Gill, *The Refugee in International Law*, n. 3 above, 196–201.

country of origin and for persons who otherwise need international protection. Since temporary protection is conceptually concerned with large numbers of persons, it is inevitable that a system of burden-sharing is seen to be part of the quantum of measures which accompany it. In a welcome note, the Treaty seeks to promote a balance of effort between Member States in receiving and bearing the consequences of receiving refugees and displaced persons.

The long term advantage brought about by the Treaty of Amsterdam is that claims to asylum and the movement and residence of refugees will be justiciable for the first time before the European Court of Justice. Ironically, the European Court of Human Rights retains a lack of direct competence on the subject of asylum.

5. CONCLUSIONS

(1) Although refugees have a distinct status in international law, restrictions affecting their movement and residence within States fall within the purview of human rights standards.

(2) Three forms of restrictions apply to refugees and asylum seekers and are subject to justification: derogations as part of provisional measures invoked in exceptional circumstances; restrictions on asylum seekers whose entry in the host State is unlawful but direct from the State of origin; and restrictions on refugees lawfully within the State. In situations of mass influx, restrictions may be placed on the movement and residence of refugees in reception areas as part of a humane public order system for managing the influx, but such restrictions must be temporary in character and should not constitute detention or internment.

(3) Restrictions may also be applied in special cases to regulate movement in designated areas or zones created especially for the residence of refugees, provided they do not deprive refugees of their liberty within or outside of those areas or zones. Moreover, restrictions should not breach other rights, such as the right to food and assistance.

(4) Restrictions which confine refugees to settlements or camps and prohibit their movement generally outside the settlements or camps are questionable and may be unjustified on grounds of reasonableness and proportionality.

(5) However, restrictions concerning the safe location of refugees are permissible where there is a danger of attack either from the country of origin, or within the receiving State. Restrictions which are placed to contain subversive activities should only apply to the movement and residence of individual refugees in relation to whom evidence of involvement in subversive activities is established.

(6) Free movement regimes in regional Communities or Unions should, in principle, benefit refugees from the constraints of territoriality. In addition, individualized forms of the persecution of persons in individual countries within West, East, and Southern Africa can be avoided by virtue of free movement away from the countries concerned to others within those regions.

(7) The objectives of market-driven communities and Unions and those of human rights are not necessarily divorced; they are identical and reconcilable, with human rights providing the underpinning values of the market so that nationals, third-country nationals, and refugees as symbols of disorder and common denominators in the application of human rights to those in need of protection, can enjoy freedom of movement and residence.

7

Derogation of Freedom of Movement

1. INTRODUCTION

States have historically derogated from the protection of human rights during times of national emergency or war. From the point of view of States, the justification for derogation—as extravagantly laid down by Peru—is that the State should take appropriate steps to safeguard its own stability and security against a form of perverse delinquency which jeopardizes and injures mankind's most highly prized individual and collective interests.[1]

Human rights standards fully acknowledge the principle of derogation but seek to limit its application according to well-defined criteria.[2] The underlying necessity for such standards is clear in any case; in principle, derogation is a form of restriction which depreciates the quality of protection accorded to human rights during states of emergency. Free movement and the ability to choose a place of residence within States is amongst those rights in respect of which derogation is permitted when a declaration of a state of emergency is in force, and national emergencies by their very nature tend to constrain the presence of persons in areas where there is danger to public safety as well as to national security. The problem extends to the treatment of civilian populations during war, obligations of occupying powers, and the legality of internment during armed conflict. However, these matters are beyond the scope of the present work and merit separate treatment.

In human rights terms the difficulty surrounding derogation lies in ensuring that when invoked, derogations do not mask a policy of perpetual abuse by way of deprivation of liberty, accompanied in certain instances by the imposition of curfews restricting internal movement, or conversely, the compulsory movement of persons.[3] Because restrictions are capable of being applied in the context of derogations, and the fact that derogations

[1] 'Report of Peru to the Human Rights Committee', *United Nations Year Book on Human Rights* (New York, 1979), 163. See also the views of Chile expressed in 'Limitations on Guarantees, Inter-American Commission for Human Rights', in Buergenthal, *Human Rights. The Inter American System*, Booklet 22.2, at 53.

[2] Article 4 of the International Covenant of Civil and Political Rights; Article 15 of the European Convention for the Protection of Human Rights and Fundamental Freedoms; Article 27 of the American Convention on Human Rights; *Legality of the Threat or Use of Nuclear Weapons*, para. 25.

[3] See, e.g., the (1996) ICJ 1. Preservation of Public Security Act (c. 57 of the Laws of Kenya).

have a far-reaching effect, it is pragmatic to consider the validity of restrictions in the context of derogations. In doing so, this chapter serves a more *ad hoc* than substantive purpose and the interested reader should take warm comfort in the standard works on derogations.[4]

However, the chapter draws a distinction between ordinary restrictions on movement and residence, and restrictions on the basis of derogations under states of emergency. Restrictions arising from derogation are legally different from ordinary restrictions on freedom of movement and residence within States. The latter envisage the existence of that right in general, and impinge on its scope on specified public interest grounds. Such restrictions may be temporary or permanent and apply ordinarily to sustain the balance between individual or group rights on the one hand, and public interests on the other. For example, prohibition of movement and residence in military locations on grounds of national security in peace-time is normal. By contrast, derogations or restrictions related to a national or public emergency have the potential or actual effect of abrogating freedom of movement and residence for the duration of the emergency.[5] The legal principles of human rights place a series of international obligations upon a State which exercises derogation. It is to those standards that the chapter will now turn.

2. STANDARDS CONCERNING DEROGATIONS

The applicable standards derive from the treaty expression of the principles of international law which govern situations of derogation.[6] They can be identified in summary as follows: the principle of exceptional threat; the principle of proclamation; the principle of notification; the principle of proportionality; the principle of non-discrimination; and the principle of consistency with international obligations.

(i) The principle of exceptional threat

The primary basis for derogation is the existence of an extremely serious exceptional threat to a State. The International Covenant on Civil and

[4] See Oraa, *Human Rights in States of Emergency in International Law* (Oxford, 1992); Chowdhury, *Rule of Law in A State of Emergency* (London, 1989); International Law Association, *Report of the Committee on Human Rights to the 58th Conference in Manila 1978* (London, 1980), 70–158, Higgins, 'Derogations Under Human Rights Treaties' (1976–77) *BYIL* 281.

[5] Higgins, 'Derogations', n. 4 above, 281.

[6] See n. 2 above; see the Human Rights Committee's General Comment 5, CCPR/C/21/Rev.1/1989. As to the role of the Committee on derogations, see McGoldrick, *The Human Rights Committee* (Oxford, 1994), ch. 7.

Political Rights[7] refers to 'a public emergency which threatens the life of the nation'. The European Convention for the Protection of Human Rights and Fundamental Freedoms[8] mentions 'war or other public emergency threatening the life of the nation', and the American Convention on Human Rights alludes to 'war, public danger or other emergency that threatens the independence or security of the state'.[9] The African Charter is silent on this issue.

Although there is a contrary opinion,[10] the practical meaning of this phrase cannot be precise since any threats to the life of a nation or nations will vary at any given time. The view taken in 1984 by the International Law Association at its meeting in Paris was that it was neither desirable nor possible to stipulate *in abstracto* what particular type or types of events will automatically constitute a public emergency within the meaning of the term. As such, each case had to be judged on its own merits, taking into account the overriding concern for the continuance of a democratic society.[11]

Nonetheless, the practical importance of delineating the content of the application of the standard behind the phrase cannot be denied for there must be objective justification of the premise for derogation. The European Court of Human Rights has stated that the natural and customary meaning of the words 'other public emergency threatening the life of the nation' is an exceptional situation of crisis or emergency which affects the whole population and constitutes a threat to the organized life of the community of which the State is composed.[12] The requirement is for the emergency to be nationwide in effect. Consequently, a local impact brought about by an emergency situation cannot qualify as a public emergency; the threat posed must be firmly to the 'organized life' of the community and it is not suggested that the life of the nation itself need be threatened with extinction. It is sufficient that 'organized life' cannot be maintained[13] owing to a breakdown of order or communications during the time of the emergency. The Inter-American Court has shown a degree of latitude towards the basis for invoking derogations. The Commission concedes that what may be permissible in one type of emergency may not be lawful in another. Beyond that, however, the Court has indicated that the lawfulness of the measures of derogation will depend upon the character, intensity, pervasiveness, and particular context of the emergency.[14]

These pronouncements show that it is an international judicial function

[7] Article 4. [8] Article 15. [9] Article 27.

[10] Oraa, *Human Rights*, n. 4 above, 14.

[11] International Law Association, *Report of the Paris Conference* (1984), 59.

[12] *Lawless* case, (1961) 1 E.H.R.R. 15–41.

[13] See Harris *et al*, *Law of the European Convention on Human Rights* (London, 1995), 491–5; Fawcett, *The Application of the European Convention on Human Rights*, 2nd edn. (Oxford, 1987), 308.

[14] Habeas Corpus in Emergency Situations, Advisory Opinion OC-8/87, 30 January 1987.

to determine whether the facts alleged to constitute an emergency satisfy legal standards and an international Court may inquire into the validity of the facts alleged to have brought about the necessity for derogation. In one of its early considerations of this matter in the *Cyprus* case[15] the European Commission declared that it was competent to examine the existence of a public danger which would justify derogation.

Later in 1961, the European Court adopted this approach in the *Lawless*[16] case. A state of emergency was proclaimed in Ireland on 8 July 1957 due to increased military activities by the Irish Republican Army and special powers of detention without trial came into force under Act No 2 1940 as a result. The applicant was detained between 13 July and 11 December 1957 without trial in a military detention camp within the Republic of Ireland. By his own admission, the applicant became a member of the Irish Republican Army in January 1956 but had left that organization in June of the same year.

In examining the issue of his detention, the Court made a direct assessment of the facts pertaining to the existence of a state of emergency in the Republic of Ireland in order to determine whether the conditions laid down for the exercise of the power of derogation were fulfilled. The Court found that the Irish Government had reasonably deduced the state of public emergency from certain facts, notably the presence of a secret army engaged in unconstitutional activities and using violence to attain its purposes in the Republic of Ireland, operations of this army outside the territory of the Republic of Ireland, which seriously jeopardized the relations of the Republic with the United Kingdom, and the steady increase in terrorist activities from the autumn of 1956. In contradistinction, the Inter-American Commission for Human Rights determined that the various situations in which the Constitution of Chile in 1980 authorized the suspension or restriction of certain rights did not meet the criterion of a threat to the nation because it made provision for the existence of a mere threat, rather than actual danger to the security of the State.[17]

In his study on the subject of states of emergency in public international law, Oraa[18] has noted that in Latin American countries, many states of emergency have been declared for security reasons without any objective justification and that this has produced gross violations of human rights. This study further shows that under international law, so-called states of emergency of a 'preventive nature' are not lawful because it is not permissible for States to derogate from human rights in order to face possible

15 176/56: 2 *Yearbook* 177.

16 (1961) 1 E.H.R.R. 15–41; see also *Brannigan and McBride v UK*, Applications No. 14533/89 and 14544/89, Report of the Commission, 3 December 1991.

17 Inter-American Commission on Human Rights, 'Limitations on Guarantees', in Buergenthal, n. 1 above, Booklet 22.2, 55.

18 Oraa, *Human Rights*, n. 4 above, 15.

exceptional situations which have not yet arisen. To constitute a threat to the life of the nation, the emergency must be present or at least imminent, its effects must involve the whole population, and the threat must be to the very existence of the nation.

Judicial inquiry into the circumstances of an emergency constitutes the pure judicial function of assessing the justification for derogation by reference to objective criteria set by human rights. In the case of *Denmark, Norway, and Netherlands v Greece*,[19] the Commission was able to determine that the evidence tendered by the military regime in Greece did not disclose a public emergency threatening the life of the nation in April 1967. And in the *Lawless* case, the Court pointed out that in considering whether a particular restriction or derogation is necessary or strictly required, the judgement of the respondent government is not accepted as conclusive.

(ii) The principle of proclamation

It is essential that a state of emergency must be officially proclaimed or declared. Official proclamation of the existence of a state of emergency is an important prerequisite to the justification of derogations under international standards concerning states of emergency.[20] Official proclamation of the existence of a state of emergency signals the existence of grave danger to the State, and shows the justification for derogating from certain rights. The *rationale* behind the requirement for proclamation is to reduce the incidence of *de facto* states of emergency by obliging States to declare publicly that an emergency exists under procedures set by domestic law and measured against international obligations. This may seem to be a straightforward obligation but in fact, in General Comment 5, the Human Rights Committee lamented that it was unclear from many States whether states of emergency had been officially declared.

(iii) The principle of notification

International obligations in the matter of human rights concern other States generally. The requirement for States which derogate from human rights during states of emergencies to notify other State parties to a relevant human rights treaty reflects the concern shared by other States in the manner in which human rights obligations are performed. The principle of notification requires States which have derogated from human rights to inform other State parties through an established intermediary of the

[19] *Greek* case (1969) 12 *Yearbook of the European Convention* 33–43.
[20] Article 4(1) of the Covenant on Civil and Political Rights 1966.

reasons for the state emergency, the measures taken pursuant to the state of emergency, and the date on which the derogation will terminate.[21] Notification ought to be sent in good time and must include derogated rights or provisions and the reasons for derogation. The Committee on Human Rights has explained that when a public emergency which threatens the life of the nation arises and it is officially proclaimed, the State party to the Covenant on Civil and Political Rights is also under an obligation to inform the other State parties immediately, through the Secretary General of the United Nations, of the derogations it has made, including the reasons therefore and the date on which the derogations are terminated.[22]

It would seem that the notice of proclamation must be sufficient and reasonable, and the communication of notice without delay is an element to take into account in determining the sufficiency of information regarding the measures of derogation. The sufficiency of notice may be questioned, and it is a judicial function to inquire into the sufficiency of the notice of proclamation. In the *Greek* case, the European Commission concluded that Greece failed to meet fully the requirements for sufficient notice under the European Convention on the grounds that:

(a) it did not communicate to the Secretary General of the Council of Europe the texts of a number of legislative measures taken in the wake of proclaiming a state of emergency;
(b) it failed to provide the Secretary General with full information of administrative measures taken particularly with regard to the detention of persons without court order; and
(c) it did not communicate to the Secretary General the reasons for the measures of derogation until four months after such measures were first taken.

(iv) The principle of non-derogability

Certain rights are recognized as not being subject to derogation during national emergencies. These are rights considered to be absolutely fundamental and indispensable to the protection of the human being. These are the right to life, freedom from torture, and other inhuman and degrading treatment or punishment, the right to be free from slavery or servitude and non-retroactive application of penal laws.[23] The norms of *jus cogens* are clearly involved here.

[21] Article 4(3) of the International Covenant on Civil and Political Rights; Article 15(3) of the European Convention for the Protection of Human Rights and Fundamental Freedoms, and Article 27(3) of the American Convention on Human Rights.

[22] General Comment 5, n. 6 above.

[23] For detail, see Oraa, *Human Rights*, n. 4 above, 136–49.

(v) The principle of proportionality

Actual measures taken by a State to derogate or restrict rights of persons generally must be proportionate to the necessity for derogation or restriction. The International Covenant on Civil and Political Rights, and the European Convention for the Protection of Human Rights and Fundamental Freedoms permit derogations only to the 'extent required by the exigencies of the situation'. To this stipulation, the American Convention on Human Rights adds, 'to the extent and for the period of time strictly required'.

The cornerstone of the requirement for proportionality is that even if there is a state of emergency, measures of derogation must be limited to the strict requirements of the exigencies of the situation. Thus the Inter-American Commission has elaborated that the words 'to the extent required' refer to the criterion of proportionality, while the words 'for the period of time' refer to the criterion of temporariness. In the opinion of the Commission, any restrictions or suspension of rights must be limited in time, and be appropriate to the seriousness of the situation which triggers the adoption of such measures.[24] This stand was reiterated by the Commission in its *Report on the Situation of Human Rights in Argentina*[25] in which it tritely observed that the suspension of rights should be applied only in so far as it is necessary for specific time periods, and solely for the purpose of correcting the reasons of the suspension. The suspension or restriction of a right by derogation cannot therefore continue indefinitely, especially when the affected right concerns personal freedom.

Whether or not measures of derogation are proportionate to the exigencies of the situation is a matter which requires the application of a legal standard to the existing facts on which the emergency is alleged to exist. In the case of Chile, the Commission examined the facts surrounding the proclamation of the state of emergency and then concluded that Chile had, in practice, been living under states of emergency since the date of the military coup on 11 September 1973. The Commission was of the view that this permanent state of emergency contravened the provisions of the international instruments which require states of emergency to be temporary.[26] A similar decision was arrived at by the European Commission for Human Rights in the *de Becker* case.[27] In this case, the European Commission stated that continued derogation of rights would not be justifiable under the Convention after the state of emergency would have ceased.

[24] Buergenthal, *The Inter-American System*, n. 1 above, Booklet 22.3, at 8.

[25] OEA/Ser.L/V/II.49, doc.19, corr.1, 11 April 1980, in Buergenthal, *The Inter-American System*, n. 1 above, at 95.

[26] Inter-American Commission for Human Rights, 'Limitations on Guarantees' in Buergenthal, n. 1 above, at 55.

[27] See Report of the Commission, n. 16 above, at 115.

The European Court for Human Rights has developed criteria for measuring the extent to which derogation is strictly required. One criterion is that there must be a proven inadequacy or breakdown of the ordinary means of law enforcement. The implication is that where the lawfulness of derogation is in issue, the State which invokes measures of derogation must prove that ordinary restrictions on the freedom of internal movement and residence are inadequate to contain the situation at hand.

When the Court applied this criterion in the case of *Lawless*, it was satisfied that the ordinary law had proved unable to check the growing danger which threatened the Republic of Ireland in 1957; and, further, that the ordinary criminal courts, or even the special criminal courts or military courts, could not suffice to restore peace and order. This led the Court to conclude that the administrative detention of individuals suspected of intending to take part in terrorist activities appeared to be a measure required by the circumstances, although it was a grave measure.

Another criterion is that there should exist safeguards against the abuse of powers, particularly in cases involving administrative detention. In the *Lawless* case, the Court welcomed the fact that there was constant supervision by Parliament over the exercise of the powers of emergency, along with the possibility that cases of detention would be referred to a Detention Commission empowered to order the release of detainees. However, in *Brogan v UK*,[28] the majority of the Court remained unpersuaded that the background of terrorism was justification for extending periods of administrative detention without judicial supervision.

(vi) The principle of non-discrimination

The derogation of rights during periods of national emergencies, and the measures taken to deal with the emergency must not discriminate on grounds of race, colour, sex, language, religion, or social origin.[29] Any difference of treatment in this respect must be justified. However, it is not entirely clear whether the grounds on which non-discrimination is prohibited in situations of emergency include those of political or other opinion, national origin, property, birth or other status under the Covenant on Civil and Political Rights. While the possibility remains that restrictions on these grounds would appear, on the face of it, to be legitimately permissible during states of emergency, the Committee's General Comment indicates only that a State party may not take discriminatory measures on a number of grounds.

[28] (1989) 11 E.H.R.R. 117.

[29] Article 4(1) of the Covenant on Civil and Political Rights; Article 27(1) of the American Convention on Human Rights; Article 15(1) of the European Convention for the Protection of Human Rights and Fundamental Freedoms.

(vii) The principle of consistency

Measures of derogation must not conflict with a State's other obligations under international law, whether these be by treaty or customary international law. This is a wide 'catch-all' obligation providing a broad legal basis on which the powers of derogation may be measured, but its precise mode of application cannot be readily identified although the purpose is apparent.

There can be no *a priori* statement of the range of obligations which may conflict with measures of derogation. The important thing is that this obligation enables acts of the derogating State to be examined in the context of the totality of its international obligations.

3. THE LEGALITY OF DEROGATIONS IN RELATION TO INTERNAL MOVEMENT AND RESIDENCE

The case of Miskito Indians[30] best illustrates the application of the principles of derogation in the context of freedom of movement and residence within States. The facts of the case (set out in more detail above in Chapter 5) are that in 1982, approximately 8,500 Miskito Indians were relocated by the Government of Nicaragua from their communities on the Coco and Bokay rivers to the Tasba Pri settlements in Zelaya, about 60 kilometres from the border with Honduras.

The measure of relocation, however, preceded a declaration of a state of emergency by the Nicaraguan Government.[31] Before the Commission, Nicaragua explained that it had previously planned to transfer part of the Coco river population to a more fertile region protected from annual floods. Frequent incursions of counter-revolutionary bands from the Honduran side of the river had created a war situation in the zone.

Nicaragua viewed such incursions as part of an international attack on itself, presenting a growing danger to its territorial integrity and national sovereignty. The strip of territory inhabited by Miskitos was declared a high security military zone; the civilian Miskito population was trapped in the sphere of military engagement between Nicaraguan forces and the counter-revolutionary bands. Because of this situation, the Nicaraguan Government determined that the safety of Miskitos necessitated compulsory relocation, despite that the initial design to resettle the Miskitos had been intended to be implemented progressively by persuasion.

[30] IACHR, *Report on the Situation of Human Rights of a Segment of the Nicaraguan Population of Miskito Origin* (DEA/Ser./V/II.62, doc.26, 1984), 41.

[31] On 15 March 1982, Nicaragua suspended the guarantees and rights set forth in Decree No. 52 of 21 August 1979 for 30 days within certain exceptions.

The Commission sought to establish whether the compulsory relocation of the Miskitos was legally justified by the fact that there was a state of emergency in Nicaragua, even though the emergency was declared subsequent to the relocation. In doing so the Commission had to determine whether the compulsory relocation of the Miskitos was undertaken in accordance with international obligations governing derogation.

Having regard to the nature of the threat posed to Nicaragua, the Commission affirmed the application of the principle of exceptional threat, and held that there was truly a threat to the organized life of the State of Nicaragua. On this basis, the Commission found that the security of the Nicaraguan State was genuinely threatened by the incursions of the groups of the former members of the National Guard, and the declaration and maintenance of a state of emergency in Nicaragua was justifiable. Moreover, the continued penetration by armed groups into Nicaraguan territory demonstrates that there was a real and imminent threat to the security of the State. Therefore, the compulsory relocation of the Miskitos Indians was grudgingly acceptable for reasons of military necessity:

> The forced evacuation of nearly 8,500 people, in some cases in the middle of the night and by armed forces, to create a military zone is only justifiable in the absence of any other alternative to meet a serious emergency.[32]

But the Commission appeared to criticize the Nicaraguan Government for not having publicly proclaimed a state of emergency which 'would have avoided an atmosphere of terror and confusion in the relocation of Miskitos and the dramatic flight of 10,000 of them to Honduras'.[33] In relation to the issue of proportionality, the Commission maintained the view that the measures of relocation should be proportionate to the danger, both with respect to degree and duration. On the facts, the Commission held that forced movement in the circumstances was proportionate to the nature of the threat posed by the emergency. However, it also pointed out that the measure of relocation should not outlast the emergency which, when terminated, should allow the return of the civilian population to their original land if they so desired:

> In the opinion of the Commission, . . . the Miskitos who choose not to remain in the Tasba Pri once the emergency is over may return to the Coco River region, which means that the measures should be limited only to the duration of the emergency, thus meeting the other requisites established by the pertinent norms.[34]

With regard to non-discrimination, the Commission found that the relocation of Miskito Indians for military reasons was not carried out in a discriminatory manner. But the Commission cautioned that if the Miskitos

[32] IACHR, *Report on the Situation of Human Rights*, n. 30 above, 46.
[33] IACHR, *Report on the Situation of Human Rights*, n. 30 above, 21. [34] Ibid., 46.

were not helped to return to the Coco river region once the military emergency were over, their prolonged stay in Tsaba Pri would become a form of discriminatory punishment. This statement was prompted by the Commission's finding that the Nicaraguan Government considered the Miskitos to be a subordinate and suspect population who could be manipulated for military purposes. It seems the relocation of Miskitos would have been discriminatory had it been undertaken solely for this reason.

The decisions reached by the Inter-American Commission for Human Rights in this case, and the approach taken by the European Commission and Court on Human Rights in cases involving issues of derogation, suggest that the rule of *prima facie invalidity* does not apply to derogations. In other words, once a state of emergency has been proclaimed, restrictions on internal freedom of movement and residence would appear to be *prima facie* lawful. The concept of the margin of appreciation as applied by the European Court vindicates this proposition.[35]

4. THE MARGIN OF APPRECIATION

The basic idea behind the concept of the margin of appreciation is the notion of discretion which State have in appreciating or determining the circumstances in which human rights may be restricted or derogated in the national interest.[36] Merrills[37] explains the concept of the margin of appreciation as follows:

> The underlying idea is a simple one: that in respect of many matters the Convention leaves the Contracting Parties an area of discretion. However, easy as this is to state, its application in concrete situations is fraught with difficulty. Cases in which the margin of appreciation is pleaded—whether the plea is successful or not—are therefore likely to be controversial.

A variety of situations to which the concept has been applied include derogation of rights by virtue of use of emergency powers, restriction of rights on account of public interest, imposition of restrictions necessary in a democratic society, and cases involving the principle of non-discrimination.[38] As all these categories may involve restriction of movement and residence of persons, a consideration of the legal technique behind the margin of appreciation is clearly relevant.

[35] See for example, *Lawless* case, Series B, 408; *Irish* Case, Series A, No. 25, para. 207.

[36] See *Lawless* case, para. 65; Yourow, *The Margin of Appreciation in the Dynamics of European Human Rights Jurisprudence* (Dordrecht, 1996).

[37] Merrills, *The Development of International Law by the European Court of Human Rights* (Manchester, 1988), 136 and the cases referred to thereon; Harris, *Cases and Materials on International Law*, 4th edn. (London, 1991), 651.

[38] Ibid., 136.

The legal technique underlying the margin of appreciation enables the European Court of Human Rights to supervise the way in which domestic law is applied to certain categories of human rights under the regime of the European Convention. It provides a means by which the Court independently examines the evidence surrounding measures taken by European State Parties to restrict or derogate upon certain human rights in order to maintain law and order, and to sustain the public interests concerned.

The technique employed by the Court in this process is a commendable compromise for effecting a proper balance between the necessity for restrictions, and the public justification for resorting to them. While States have a margin of appreciation as a matter of domestic jurisdiction and are thus the sole judge in determining the occasion for imposing restrictions in the public interest, the matter of justification and lawfulness of the restrictions is subject to objective legal scrutiny against standards set in human rights treaty regimes. At one level, the margin of appreciation is consistent with State responsibility, but at another level, it may have the effect of avoiding the responsibility of States where the margin is determined in favour of a State to the detriment of its international human rights obligations. A crucial issue is whether the steps taken to restrict the right of movement and residence, and the conditions imposed in the manner of restriction of the right exceed, or are within the bounds of, necessity.

Regarding this issue, the pertinent questions are: were the restrictions made in accordance with, or prescribed by, law? Were they justified because they were necessary on specified public interest grounds? Were the restrictions lawful because they were reasonably proportionate to the necessity for them? In seeking answers to such questions, the technique employed by the European Court of Human Rights is helpful.

Answers to these questions depend on the conditions and circumstances obtaining at the time of the restriction or derogation in question,[39] and whether the use of restrictions is justifiable by reference to those conditions in the light of international standards governing restrictions. The principle of proportionality plays a vital role here.

As Fitzmaurice has noted:

> Very often, in applying a rule of international law, or in estimating the validity of the state action, something . . . may turn on the reasonableness of the action itself, or on the degree of reasonableness with which the action has to be carried out. In such cases the existence of special interests or particular circumstances of, for instance, an economic, social, or geographical character, may well affect, if they do not determine, the reasonableness of the action taken.[40]

[39] *Irish* case, para. 214.

[40] Fitzmaurice, 'General Principles of International Law', (1957) 92 *Recueil*, 116.

The categories of reasonableness, legitimate interests and the like are usually employed to determine the lawfulness of the measures which are taken in the public interest to restrict rights of individuals. In the *Lawless* case the Court found that the measures taken by the Irish Government were within the margin of emergency powers as the existence at the time of a public emergency threatening the life of the nation was reasonably deduced. In the *James* case[41] the Court remarked that the margin of appreciation available to the legislature in implementing social and economic policies should naturally be a wide one, and that it would respect the legislature's judgement as to what is in the public interest unless that judgement be manifestly without reasonable foundation. The width of the margin of appreciation is thus not static; it is flexible enough to be narrowed, or widened, depending upon the value of the rights concerned. That value is measured by striking a fair balance between the requirements of the public interest and the requirements for the protection of the fundamental rights of the individual or groups.[42]

Failure to strike this balance may mean that the measures adopted by a State may not be proportionately justified in the public interest, and would thus fall outside the margin of appreciation.[43] Issues relating to the lawfulness of restrictions on the movement and residence of persons within States may be determinable on this basis, but the endemic problem is how to ensure that States do not restrict the right in a manner which renders it otiose. Flexibility in its application means that the margin of appreciation cannot adequately answer this question with any degree of certainty. A certain danger inherent in this concept appears to be that it rests, in application, on *a priori* presumption in favour of State measures as falling within the margin of appreciation, much the same way as the presumption of constitutionality operates in municipal legal systems.

There is evidence for this trend. In a narrow majority decision, the basis for dissent[44] was that:

> it is part of the established jurisprudence of this court that a Contracting State is entitled to a margin of appreciation when the question whether it has committed a violation of the Convention is under review.

If such a view came to represent the jurisprudence of the Court, the difficulty presented by it is obvious. There would be a heavy burden on the part of an applicant to rebut the presumption of legality in favour of the measures taken by a State. Ideally, the question whether a State acted within the margin of appreciation should be pleaded by that State. The onus of discharging the burden of proof, i.e., of showing that a State took

[41] *James v United Kingdom* (1986) 8 E.H.R.R. 123, para. 46.
[42] Merrills, *The Development*, n. 37 above, 148–54. [43] Ibid., 142.
[44] Dissenting Opinion of Judge Zekia, *Guzzardi v Italy* (1981) 61 I.L.R. 324.

measures justified in the public interest to restrict certain rights must lie on the State at the commencement of the proceedings without any aid of entitlement or presumption operating in its favour.

5. CONCLUSIONS

(1) Subject to justification, a presumption of legality operates *prima facie* in favour of measures of derogation taken by a State which has proclaimed a national state of emergency.

(2) Restrictions on internal movement and residence on the basis of derogations are justified by the existence of an exceptional threat to the life of the nation, but they must be proportionate to the threat posed by the emergency, and be compatible with a State's obligations under general international law, including the principle of non-discrimination. These standards constitute conditions for the validity of derogations.

(3) The significance of such standards is such that international tribunals are competent to inquire into the circumstances of the emergency to establish the existence of a threat to the nation, and whether the measures of derogation are proportionate to the exigencies of the situation.

(4) As part of the proof of the proportionality of derogations, the derogating State must show that ordinary limitations to freedom of movement and residence were inadequate to contain the emergency situation.

(5) Moreover, there should exist adequate safeguards for supervising and reviewing measures of derogation to safeguard against the general abuse of rights as well as the use of restrictions.

8

Conclusions

The scope of freedom of movement within States, and the range of matters that it relates to are undoubtedly broader than the treatment presented in this monograph. Internal migration, the relation between internal movement and economic social and cultural rights, and the position of persons displaced within States owing to civil strife, are some of the contemporary problems pressing for analysis within the framework of freedom of movement and residence within States.

However, these and many other problems call for the application of the standards concerning freedom of movement and residence in specific contexts but there is great merit in providing a foundation for the analysis of the content of the standards applicable to freedom of movement in general and in the light of specific categories of persons and groups within States as presented in this work.

It has to be reiterated that the extent to which freedom of movement can be protected depends in large measure on the legality of the restrictions placed upon it. Accordingly, and given that each of the foregoing chapters has carried a summary conclusion, the conclusions presented here focus upon the legality of such restrictions. Their range and the use to which they are put to regulate and control freedom of movement and residence include, but are not limited to, monitoring and regulating general movement and residence, restrictions designed to entrench a policy of racial discrimination, internal banishment, forcible relocation, protection of minority and indigenous groups, as well as refugees. There could be others.

The penultimate point is that whatever the nature of the restriction in question, the standards governing any type of restriction of movement remain substantively the same as formulated in human rights treaties, and the system of international legal protection of human rights provides standards external to States as well as independent legal techniques for assessing the legality of the conduct of States in matters of freedom of movement.

By its very nature, freedom of movement and residence within States is prone to regulation by the State, and the main issue is to determine the legality of the margins of protection within which the control of movement can be justified or permitted. The applicable standards can be found in treaties as evidence of generally accepted standards on freedom of movement and residence within States. These standards may be summarized as follows:

(1) Generally:

(a) restrictions must be deemed necessary or justified on the basis of specific grounds of public interest;
(b) restrictions must be provided for by means of enacted law which prescribes their application and defines the grounds upon which they are applicable;
(c) the modality of the restrictions ought to be consistent with the grounds enumerated in human rights treaties and with the enjoyment of other human rights on the basis of proportionality;
(d) the right of movement and residence may be derogated from temporarily in exceptional situations involving states of emergency, but specific standards apply in the event of derogation;
(e) restrictions and derogations are subject to the principle of non-discrimination at all times.

(2) Restrictions based on racial discrimination are prohibited on the basis of the status of non-racial discrimination as a norm of *jus cogens*.

(3) The essential character of restrictions is contrary to the presumption of regularity, and the logic of the discussion presented in this book suggests that there is, in general, a *prima facie* presumption, though not a conclusive presumption, operating against restrictions.

(4) This presumption arises from the general prohibition on the imposition of restrictions on the movement and residence of persons within States as evidenced by the standards contained in Article 12(3) of the Covenant on Civil and Political Rights: 'The above mentioned rights (in reference to the freedom of international movement and internal movement and residence) shall not be subject to any restrictions'. The generality of this prohibition seeks to preserve the content of freedom of movement and residence, so that it cannot be interpreted restrictively.

(5) However that may be, there are situations in which restrictions are desirable to protect certain interests, whether of the community as a whole, or of particular groups within the State. This can be done by invoking restrictions as exceptions to the general prohibition against the restriction of freedom of movement in general.

(6) Efforts in international law to subject restrictions to effective legal controls in the context of human rights standards must be directed at the justification for restricting movement and residence, and the proportionality of the measures taken to protect the public interest in question.

(7) In challenging restrictions, the pertinent questions are: is a given restriction acceptable on the basis of necessity? Is the restriction proportionate to the public interest sought to be protected? Does the public interest ground in question justify limitation of movement and residence? Does the restriction lead to the violation of other rights?

(8) Although restrictions on freedom of movement and residence may vary in time and place, and in accordance with interests and needs of a given State, they may not be used either to erode the substance of the freedom of movement, or to deny the enjoyment of other internationally recognized rights.

Bibliography

ANKUMAH, E., *The African Commission on Human and Peoples' Rights* (The Hague, 1996).

BELLO, E., 'The African Charter on Human and Peoples Rights: A Legal Analysis', (1985 V *Recueil* 70).

BROWNLIE, I., *Basic Documents on Human Rights*, 3rd edn. (Oxford, 1992).

——*Principles of Public International Law*, 5th edn. (Oxford, 1998).

——'The Rights of Peoples in Modern International Law', in Crawford, *The Rights of Peoples* (Oxford, 1988).

——*Treaties and Indigenous Peoples* (Oxford, 1992)..

BOSSUYT, M., *Guide to the Travaux Preparatoires to the International Covenant on Civil and Political Rights* (Dordrecht, 1987).

BUERGENTHAL, N., *Human Rights. The Inter American System*, 6 vols, continuing.

CAPOTORTI, F., *Study on the Rights of Persons Belonging to Ethnic, Religious and Linguistic Minorities.* E/CN.4/Sub. 2/384/Rev.1 (1977) (New York, 1979).

COBO, J., *Study of the Problem of the Discrimination Against Indigenous Populations*, E/C.N.4/Sub.2/1986/7.

Council of Europe, *Digest of Strasbourg Case Law Relating to the European Convention on Human Rights* (1985).

CRAWFORD, J. (ed.), *The Rights of Peoples* (Oxford, 1988).

CHOWDHURRY, S., *Rule of Law in A State of Emergency* (London, 1989).

DUGARD, J., *Human Rights and the South African Legal Order* (New Jersey, 1978).

ELIAS, T., 'The Doctrine of Inter-temporal Law' (1980) 74 *AJIL* 285.

FALK, R., 'The Rights of Peoples (In Particular Indigenous Peoples)' in Crawford, *The Rights of Peoples* (Oxford, 1988).

FAWCETT, J., *The Application of the European Convention on Human Rights*, 2nd edn. (Oxford, 1987).

GOODWIN-GILL, G., *International Law and the Movement of Persons Between States* (Oxford, 1978).

——*The Refugee in International Law* (Oxford, 1996).

GRAHL-MADSEN, A., *The Status of Refugees in International Law*, 2 vols (Leyden, 1966).

HANSEN, A., and SMITH, O. (eds.), *Involuntary Migration and Resettlement: The Problems and Responses of Dislocated People* (Benlder, 1982).

HARRIS, D., *Cases and Materials on International Law*, 5th edn. (London, 1998).

——O'BOYLE, M., and WARBRICK, C., *Law of the European Convention on Human Rights* (London, 1995).

HATHAWAY, J., *The Law of Refugee Status* (London, 1991).

HENKIN, L., *The International Bill of Rights. The Covenant on Civil and Political Rights* (New York, 1981).

HIGGINS, R., 'Derogations Under Human Rights Treaties' (1976–77) *BYIL* 281.

——*Problems and Process: International Law and How We Use it* (Oxford, 1994).

——'The Contribution of the Committee on Human Rights', in Dinstein (ed.)

and Tabory (Ass. ed.), *International Law at a Time of Perplexity* (Dordrecht, 1989).

HIGGINS, R., 'The Right in International Law of an Individual to Enter, Stay, and Leave a Country', (1973) 49:3 *International Affairs*, 341–57.

HUNNUN, H., *The Right To Leave and Return in International Law and Practice* (Dordrecht, 1981).

IACHR, *Report on the Situation of Human Rights of a Segment of the Nicaraguan Population of Miskito Origin* (DEA/Ser./V/II.62, doc 26, 1984).

——*Basic Documents Pertaining to the Inter-American System* (Washington, 1996).

——*Annual Report of the Inter-American Commission on Human Rights* (Washington, 1996).

——*Annual Report of the Inter-American Court on Human Rights* (Washington, 1996).

INGLES, J., *Study of the Right of Everyone To Leave Any Country, Including His Own, And to Return to His Country*, E/CN.4/Sub.2/220.

JAGERSKIOLD, S., 'The Freedom of Movement' in Henkin (ed.), *The International Bill of Rights. The Covenant on Civil and Political Rights* (New York, 1981).

JENNINGS, R., and WATTS, A., *Oppenheim's International Law*, 9th edn., 2 vols. (London, 1992).

KINGSBURY, N., *Indigenous Peoples in International Law* (D.Phil Thesis, Oxford, 1990).

KISS, A., 'Permissible Limitations on Right', in Henkin (ed.), *The International Bill of Rights. The Covenant On Civil and Political Rights* (New York, 1981).

LAUTERPACHT, H., *International Law and Human Rights* (London, 1950).

LAWSON, E., *Encyclopedia of Human Rights* (Washington, 1991).

MCGOLDRICK, B., *The Human Rights Committee* (Oxford, 1991).

MCKEAN, W., *Equality and Discrimination under International Law* (Oxford, 1983).

MARTIN, B. (ed.), *The New Asylum Seekers: Refugee Law in the 1980s* (Dordrecht, 1988).

MELANDER, G., and NOBEL, P. (eds), *African Refugees and the Law* (Uppsala, 1978).

MERON, T., *Human Rights and Humanitarian Norms as Customary Law* (Oxford, 1989).

——(ed.), *Human Rights and International Law: Legal and Policy Issues*, 2 vols (Oxford, 1984).

——(ed.), *Human Rights: Law Making in the United Nations* (Oxford, 1986).

——'The Meaning and Reach of the International Covention on the Elimination of All Forms of Racial Discrimination' (1985) *AJIL* 283.

MERRILLS, J., *The Development of International Law By the European Court of Human Rights* (Manchester, 1988).

MUNTARBHORN, V., *The Status of Refugees in Asia* (Oxford, 1992).

ORAA, J., *Human Rights in States of Emergency in International Law* (Oxford, 1992).

ORTIZ, R. D., *Indians of the Americas: Human Rights and Self-Determination* (London, 1984).

PLENDER, R., *International Migration Law*, 2nd edn. (Dordrecht, 1988).

——*Right of Asylum* (Dordrecht, 1990).

RAMCHARAN, B. G., 'Equality and Non-Discrimination', in Henkin (ed.), *The International Bill of Rights. The International Covenant on Civil and Political Rights* (New York, 1981).

SCHACHTER, O., 'General Course in Public International Law', (1982) V Recueil 9–376.

SOHN, L., 'The Rights of Minorities', in Henkin (ed.), *The International Bill of Rights. The International Covenant on Civil and Political Rights* (New York, 1981).

STEINER, H., and ALTON, P., *International Human Rights in Context: Law Politics and Morals* (Oxford, 1996).

THORNBERRY, P., *International Law and the Rights of Minorities* (Oxford, 1991).

United Nations, *Definition and Classification of Minorities* (New York, 1950).

Index